"When the church divides over ..., ..., that Jesus can't pray effectively, and that the Holy Spirit is a slave to social pressure. Do we really want to do that before our friends and neighbors? Didn't Jesus pray that we would be one 'so that the world might know that you have sent me'?"

Charles Drew

Praise for *Surprised by Community*

"The evangelical church's disproportionate concern with power politics has all too often been a detriment to the spread of the gospel and the peace of the church. Charlie Drew puts political action in its proper place—charting a biblical course in which earthly politics is put into perspective by the Kingdom of God and reminding believers of Christian teachings about politics that transcend the issues of the moment. This book is a needed antidote to the worldliness of much Christian political involvement, whether of the conservative or liberal variety. It should be required teaching in our churches!"

William Brewbaker, Professor of Law, University of Alabama;
Ruling Elder, Trinity Presbyterian Church, Tuscaloosa, AL

"To succeed in making a God-honoring impact in the world, the Christian must understand the nuances of Scripture and acknowledge the complexity of the endeavor. Charles Drew's *Surprised by Community* is a tremendous aid to those who seek to promote the will of God."

Matthew Bennett, Founder and President, The Christian Union

"This is a gem of a book and is easily one of the best things I've read on Christian citizenship and public responsibility. Not only that, but it's written in an incisive, clear, pastoral tone and the measured tenor couldn't be more appropriate. A fabulous book it is, and I'll be commending it to one and all."

Garnette Cadogan, Freelance writer

"Over the past thirty years we have seen a renewed concern among American evangelicals for political and social concerns. Much of this has been long overdue and valid. But Charles Drew, in this important book, raises urgent and sobering cautions. Written by someone with a keen mind and a pastor's heart, he fears important truths have been compromised and the good news of the gospel has been politicized. This is bad news for the church and for society. This book is timely and we need to heed the course corrections the author recommends."

The Late Michael Cromartie, Vice President,
Ethics and Public Policy Center, Washington, DC

"This book is a much-needed and practical guide in a much-ignored sphere of Christian discipleship. Can evangelicals be constructive in politics without being combative with each other? Charlie Drew gives us the principles that will help us build our country, our witness, and the spiritual maturity of the church."

Dr. Joel C. Hunter, Senior Pastor, Northland –
A Church Distributed, Orlando, FL

"Charles Drew has given us something that is lacking in so much discussion about the Church and politics: insight. He sees that those on the religious right and left need to understand how much they each imitate, rather than challenge, the culture they seek to change. Both need a whole new way of framing the issues. The worn-out and extreme vocabularies of both have proven unproductive and even irresponsible for Christians who understand their Bible enough to know that the City of Man is shaped by the City of God it will become. Christians are not those who react and polarize, but those who live in grace and who are faithfully present in their callings."

Dr. Joseph "Skip" Ryan, former Chancellor,
Redeemer Seminary, Dallas, TX

"Charles Drew provides practical answers to the Christian political and cultural environment. *Surprised by Community* should be a standard text in Christian schools' civic curriculum."

John Seel, PhD; President, Transcend Entertainment;
Former Headmaster, the Cambridge School of Dallas

"This is clearly not a 'Republican' or 'Democrat' book. Rather, it is a self-consciously Christian and biblical approach. Since Christians (including myself!) have trouble thinking beyond ready-made political identities, this alone makes the book a must-read. A variety of practical considerations are discussed, but its greatest contribution is in helping Christians sharpen their thinking in ways that apply to ANY political topic."

Rev. Kenneth Shomo, Associate Pastor, New Covenant Church,
Virginia Beach, VA

"I cannot imagine a handier guide for anyone who struggles to navigate the treacherous waters of politics, church, and the Christian life in this contentious era. Drawing on his experience as a pastor of several diverse congregations, Charles Drew offers timely counsel on the difference between our political engagements as individuals and the proper role of the church, as well as many other vexing issues. Genial and profound, *Surprised by Community* belongs on every list of the very best recent books on Christianity and politics."

David Skeel, S. Samuel Arsht Professor of Law,
University of Pennsylvania Law School;
Ruling Elder, Tenth Presbyterian Church, Philadelphia, PA

"This is a wise and refreshingly moderate book. Political discussions among Christians tend to generate more heat than light. This book generates light—I understand both my obligations as a citizen and my obligations as a believer better for having read it."

The Late William Stuntz, the Former Henry J. Friendly
Professor of Criminal Law, Harvard Law School

SURPRISED
BY
COMMUNITY

Republicans and Democrats
in the Same Pew

CHARLES D. DREW

Copyright © 2019 by Charles D. Drew. All rights reserved.
Published 2019
First edition © 2000 by Charles D. Drew, *A Public Faith: Bringing Personal Faith to Public Issues* (NavPress)
Second edition © 2012 by Charles D. Drew, *Body Broken: Can Republicans and Democrats Sit in the Same Pew?* (New Growth Press).

All Scripture quotations, unless otherwise indicated, are taken from
THE HOLY BIBLE, NEW INTERNATIONAL VERSION®, NIV®
Copyright © 1973, 1978, 1984, 2011 by Biblica, Inc™
Used by permission. All rights reserved worldwide.

ISBN 978-1-54396-887-3 (ebook)
ISBN 13: 978-1-936768-30-1
ISBN 10: 1-936768-30-5

Library of Congress Cataloging-in-Publication Data

Drew, Charles D., 1950–
Surprised by Community: Republicans and Democrats in the Same Pew/
Charles D. Drew.
Rev. ed. of: Body Broken: Can Republicans and Democrats Sit in the Same
Pew? and A Public Faith: Bringing Personal Faith to Public Issues.
Includes bibliographical references and index.

ISBN-978-1-54396-886-6
ISBN-13: 978–1-936768–30–1 (alk. paper)
ISBN-10: 1–936768–30–5 (alk. paper)
1. Christianity and politics—United States. I. Drew, Charles D., 1950-
Public faith. II. Title.
Body broken
BR526.D74 2012
261.70973—dc23 2011034614
Printed in the United States of America

For James I. Packer
who has graciously taught us to look for common ground
without abandoning conviction

CONTENTS

Introduction

Two weeks before the 2016 national election our church in New York City held a church-wide forum featuring a discussion of some of the contents of this book followed by presentations by two congregational members, one who was a Republican and the other who was a Democrat. After some opening remarks by me, the panelists declared how they were going to vote followed by an explanation of their positions. They then entertained questions from each other, from me, and from the congregation. Following the panel we divided the congregation into discussion groups and invited them to talk about a "hot topic" together using certain guidelines and to close their discussion in prayer. The gracious tone of the panelists, their thoughtful engagement with Scripture and each other, and the nuance of their thinking—combined with the peaceable group discussions that followed—demonstrated that the church really can be a political surprise—a place where people can deeply disagree and yet still love each other.

Here are some of the responses from parishioners who attended that event:

- What I found comforting during the workshop was knowing that I could voice my thoughts, and, even if someone disagreed with me, I could still find them, post-election, and hug them (figuratively and literally). The church is truly my family… Churches that do not offer this leave members quietly tired and terrified. ("Jocelyn": A staff person of an anti-trafficking nonprofit)

- I can't overstate how much I would recommend workshops like this in a church setting. I found it helpful to hear perspectives from opposite sides of the political spectrum, in a format that did not promote one candidate over another, but rather respectfully highlighted issues of significance to the panelists with a humble explanation of why they believed one candidate, or party, better supported the ends they sought. I relished the opportunity to pray for our divided nation together. ("William"—A graduate student at the School of International and Public Affairs, Columbia University)

The church can be a social surprise. It can be a safe place to talk about politics. I am convinced, in fact, that the church can be the safest place in the world to argue about politics. I am also persuaded that it must be.

Why do I say this? First, because Jesus died to unite us, demolishing by the cross the "dividing wall(s) of hostility" that come between us, including the political ones (see Ephesians 2). Secondly, because Jesus prays that we will "be one just as he and the Father are" (see John 17:22): he prays that the quality of our love will mirror the quality of the love that has always been in the Trinity. Thirdly, because the Spirit of Jesus lives in us. Let me put the matter negatively: When the church blows up, or even divides, over politics, we "prove" that the cross didn't take, that Jesus can't pray effectively, and that the Holy Spirit is a slave to social pressure. Do we really want to do that before our friends and neighbors?

Sometimes we fight because we are small minded, nasty, and afraid. But often we fight because we honestly disagree over the best way to love our neighbors as ourselves. Such honest disagreements shouldn't surprise us. Our world is as complicated and broken as we are, and our very best fixes are bound to be flawed: they can't possibly cover every contingency and they are often blind to people and problems that we cannot or will not see.

But I want us to believe that we can disagree without doing what the world around us does—shattering our relationships and going our separate ways. The church is going to outlast the NRA and the ACLU, and we get to give people a foretaste right now of that great hope through the way that we manage our differences.

I say "manage our differences" because we mustn't pretend they aren't there. Pretending may spare us some discomfort, but it isolates us from each other, sometimes over matters that matter deeply to us. We have to learn how to talk honestly, engage differently, and yet still stay together. When we pull this off, we get to be winsome social miracles, communities that sociologists and political pundits simply cannot explain. We get to be such a welcome surprise in our polarized times that cynical and lonely friends (and enemies, too) begin seriously to wonder about the Person we claim to know and love. We get, in other words, to be living and convincing answers to Jesus' long-standing prayer that we love each other the way he and his Father do "*so that the world might know* that the Father has sent [him]" (John 17:23).

Much has happened politically in our country since the summer of 1999 when the first iteration of this book (*A Public Faith*, NavPress) appeared. We have had eight years of a Republican administration, led by a president of strong evangelical faith. We have entered and ended a war with Iraq whose initial goals were met quickly but which lingered with much loss of life all around. We have entered and passed through the worst financial crisis since the Great Depression. We have seen eight years under the administration of a Democrat, this one (to the astonishment of many) an African American. In 2016 we saw a swing back to the right with the election of a Republican president and congress. As I write in December 2018 the pendulum has swung (lurched?) yet again as the House has regained a Democratic majority. Accompanying these swings (and, some would say, leading up to them) we have embarked upon a season of polarizing behavior and discourse the likes of which surpasses that of the Watergate era.

The church, certainly the Protestant church, has not managed this polarization very well. Theologically progressive Protestants are increasingly finding their home in progressive politics per se and are simply leaving the church. Theologically traditional Protestants ("Evangelicals") experience a different dynamic. They are "church people" at odds with other "church people" over politics.

"Evangelical" has drifted from its moorings in theology and found its new harbor in the politics of the right. This has been fine for some, whose grief over the normalizing of abortion, same sex marriage, and secularized public life gathers solace from a tradition that has resisted such normalizations. But it has been deeply disturbing for those who share the creeds of the old evangelical faith, but cannot identify that faith with a political agenda that seems to care so little for the environment, the underserved, growing wealth disparity, and egregious sexual misconduct: many of them no longer use "evangelical" to describe themselves.[1] These two groups don't talk much with each other, even though they affirm the same theology. They find themselves in different churches. Or, they find themselves in the same church but never talk politics because they are afraid of the rancor to which such talk will likely lead.

This book, like its second iteration (*Body Broken*, New Growth Press, 2012), is designed to help us get past that fear and to do a better job loving God and our neighbors *together*. It assumes that we love the Lord, his Word, and each other, while recognizing that we need help developing that third love more fully. It assumes that loving each other better is essential to our mission.

Let me describe my approach. We often make the mistake of running to God for answers before we have allowed him to teach us how best to frame our questions. We come with our wrongheaded agenda when what we need is a radical transformation of perspective. As a protection against this tendency, I have ordered my writing (for the most part) around the Bible rather than around issues (issues come and go, but God's Word abides). We want to be patient rather than impatient children, gathering quietly in the Father's study to hear him out, rather than dragging him by the hand to and from the rooms of our choosing.

Chapters one and two identify our misdirected worship as the deepest cause for the heat in our political disagreements and call us, by way of an antidote, to fresh trust in God's sovereign rule. Chapter three endeavors to clarify, on the basis of the Great Commission and 1 Timothy 2:1–6, the priorities of the church (as distinguished from those of individual Christians) in public life. Chapter four considers the meaning of the Apostle Peter's assertion that we are "foreigners and exiles." Chapters five, six, and seven explore the ramifications of Jesus' remarkable command in Mark 12:17 to "give back to Caesar what is Caesar's and to God what is God's." Chapters eight and nine explore a series of approaches for effecting social and political change, approaches that can help reduce the heat of our political differences by suggesting courses of action that lie outside the polarizing world of power politics. The final chapter (new to this volume) offers practical suggestions on how we can do a better job talking about politics at church.

At the end of each chapter you will find some questions to help you explore and apply the ideas of the chapter more deeply. You may want to tackle them on your own, but you might do better discussing them with a group of friends.

I include three documents in the appendix. The first is the Williamsburg Charter, drafted at the time of our Constitution's bicentennial to celebrate and reaffirm the meaning of religious freedom in our pluralistic day. Signed by a broad spectrum of Americans, the charter has helped me immensely as I have wrestled with the issues addressed in this book. The second, titled "Christian Citizenship," contains the text of a document we developed and distributed for a time at the Three Village Church, a parish where I served for twelve years. The third is a portion of the vision statement of Emmanuel Presbyterian Church, a congregation in New York City that I started in 2000. I offer the latter two pieces as illustrations of churches seeking to come to grips with their public responsibility, hoping that they will induce better efforts.

Thanks are due to the late Charles Colson whose *Kingdoms in Conflict* motivated and enlightened me. Those who are aware of the work of Os Guinness, James Hunter, and John Seel will recognize their influence as well. I am particularly grateful to the elders and members of the Three Village Church and Emmanuel Church, who kindly granted me the time that made this project possible.

The LORD reigns, let the earth be glad; let the distant shores rejoice. Clouds and thick darkness surround him; righteousness and justice are the foundation of his throne. Fire goes before him and consumes his foes on every side. His lightning lights up the world; the earth sees and trembles. The mountains melt like wax before the LORD, before the Lord of all the earth. The heavens proclaim his righteousness, and all peoples see his glory. All who worship images are put to shame, those who boast in idols—worship him, all you gods!

Zion hears and rejoices and the villages of Judah are glad because of your judgments, LORD. For you, LORD, are the Most High over all the earth; you are exalted far above all gods. Let those who love the LORD hate evil, for he guards the lives of his faithful ones and delivers them from the hand of the wicked. Light shines on the righteous and joy on the upright in heart. Rejoice in the LORD, you who are righteous, and praise his holy name. (Psalm 97)

Chapter 1

FIRST PRINCIPLES

We are bound to disagree over politics, not just in the culture but in the church as well. I bump into this reality all the time. One such occasion occurred in early 2009 when I had two very different appointments back to back. The first was with a leader in my church who wondered why we did not talk more forcefully about abortion and homosexuality. He wondered why we were more likely to speak out on trendy New York City issues like justice and mercy than to speak out and even act on the issues he was concerned about. He wondered why, for example, if we were prepared to sponsor a march against hunger, we were not also prepared to sponsor a protest in front of an abortion clinic.

I met next with a Christian graduate student at Columbia University. She told me that she had begun to drift away from Christian community because, as she put it, "I am beginning to find that the people I agree with theologically are the people I disagree with socially." The issues for her were, interestingly, the same as those mentioned in my first appointment—abortion and homosexuality, but especially the latter. She was in a different place on those issues. She was not gay herself, but she had a number of close friends who were, and her love for them made her feel at odds, given her prior church experience, with the Christian community. She was confused about what the Bible had to say about committed homosexual partnerships, and she was struggling over what she would do if she became convinced that the Lord forbade them. We talked about many things—about the false choice the culture often presents (one either must completely accept the gay lifestyle or one must admit to homophobia), about the different views Christians hold on the issue, about the tendency in the evangelical world to elevate certain sins over others (homosexual sin over heterosexual sin; or sexual sins over other types of sin, like greed or gossip), about the fact that there are different legitimate strategies for nudging our culture in the direction of sexual health, about the difference between struggling with sin and embracing sin, and about the difference between homosexual inclination and homosexual behavior.

I came away from the second appointment thankful and perplexed (more later on my perplexity). I was thankful that this young person had felt comfortable talking to me, for I am "the church" by virtue of my role as a pastor. I could not help but think that she approached me because our church did not, in its public face, fit the stereotype that she had begun to react to. And I think she went away heartened by the discovery that we were keen to keep our "front door" open for serious, honest, and gentle discussion.

Tensions in My Own Mind

We are bound to disagree, not only over issues, but over which issues to "go public" on. Committed Christians, sometimes in the same church, sometimes in the leadership of the same church, can easily find themselves at odds with one another on these sorts of issues.

Such tensions arise not only between us but within us. I mentioned that I came away from the second appointment perplexed. The graduate student's struggles reminded me of how confused people are, especially young people, even church-raised young people like her, about God's way of wisdom when it comes to sexual matters. I found myself asking if our church's relative public silence on the issue was in fact the best policy. Certainly it helped keep our front door more widely open than it might otherwise be. It certainly gave rise to an important and nuanced discussion with one particular person that might otherwise not have happened. But what about all the others out there?

What about those in my own church who might need a lot more guidance than they realize?

Issues Change, but Disagreement Continues

As I write, everyone is talking about tax policy, healthcare, school shootings, and immigration—but not everyone in our churches agrees on what is to be done. Back in the 1980s many of the issues were different, but Christians still found plenty to argue about. Some members of my congregation rejoiced at the swing to the right. They saw the Republican triumphs in 1980 and 1984 as harbingers of moral, fiscal, and educational renewal. Others were less sanguine, pointing with dismay to the new guard's positions on, for example, gun control and the environment as huge moral blind spots. (If they had been able to see ahead into the new century, they might have been equally appalled at the financial chaos brought upon the world by the new guard's advocacy of the unregulated pursuit of wealth.) Some saw the fall of the Soviet Union as the vindication of free market capitalism and of policies aimed at its unfettered growth. Others joined Czech Republic President Václav Havel in his fear that the lifting of Soviet control would only invite new expressions of violence, not simply in the former Soviet bloc, but even at home:

> The unnatural bipolar system imposed upon the world, which concealed or directly suppressed historical differences, has collapsed. And these differences are now manifesting themselves with sudden and nearly explosive force, not just in the post-Communist world but also in the West and many other areas of the globe. I fully agree with those who see in this reality the seeds of one of the most serious threats to humanity in the coming era.[2]

Some today might argue that the "triumph" of capitalism, and the growing disparity between the rich and the poor that has accompanied it, has been one of the sources of the rise of terrorism in the new century.

Navigating Our Differences: Don't Panic

How do we navigate all these differences? Surely it is by looking to the Scriptures for perspective and guidance. I have found Psalm 97 to be very helpful in this regard. It calls our hearts back to their proper center and for that reason serves as a manifesto on "first principles" for Christian citizenship. The first of these first principles is that Christians need never panic, since our God rules everything: "The LORD reigns, let the earth be glad; let the distant shores rejoice" (Psalm 97:1).

Notice that "reigns" is a political word. It describes a king exercising dominion over his subjects, the ancient equivalent (roughly) of saying, "President so-and-so sits in the Oval Office." Of course verse 1 says much more. We elect American presidents for a brief time. Their "reign" is neither permanent, nor absolute, nor flawless, nor worldwide, whereas God's is all four. His rule causes the "*earth*" to be "glad" and the "*distant shores*" to rejoice" (emphasis added). Verse 9 declares his absolute sovereignty over all authorities, whether seen or unseen: "For you, LORD, are the Most High over all the earth; you are exalted far above all gods." What an encouragement! What a source of confidence and joy for the believer! God is in charge absolutely.

Those who bemoan the moral and social disintegration of American culture are often right. But when they speak to us in such a way as to stir up fear and panic in our hearts, they are wrong. Our God reigns, and therefore we need not—we must not—be afraid as we exercise our civic responsibilities, no matter what seems to be going on around us.

Consider the damage panic can bring. First of all, panic impairs judgment. If we give in to the voice that cries "Act now, or our great country will be forever lost!" we will find ourselves demanding easy and quick solutions to our nation's problems, when in fact there are no such solutions. Christians, more than any others, should know that no candidate, no platform, no party has all the answers. But fear makes it easy to forget this.

Panic breeds impatience not only with political process but also with people. It easily leads to browbeating and to polarization even in the church, the very place where God expects us to model the one community that will outlast all others. How quickly and tragically we accuse and demonize one another when we are afraid. Our hearts break over the killing of millions of unborn children, but are we really right to label every pro-choicer an advocate for murder and every woman who submits to abortion an accomplice in murder? What of the young woman who has been persuaded that the child within is not yet a child? (Note: God distinguishes in Scripture between premeditated killing of a person and accidental killing, a distinction which we find in our own law's distinction between murder and manslaughter. Abortion is, of course, premeditated, but for some people that act is not morally murder since they have been led to believe that what is aborted is not a person.) What of the person who votes pro-choice because she cannot see how the legal battle against abortion will succeed rather than because she is pro-abortion? Because panic cries "Do something right now, before it is too late!" it dehumanizes us in our dealings with each other. For me to understand my neighbor's motives and reasoning takes time, the very thing panic cannot stand.

Panic can be used to justify falsehood. Some people, fearful of a religious takeover, have lifted Jefferson's "wall of separation" idea out of its historical context and used it, dishonestly, to justify the silencing of the religious voice in every public place and discussion. (The language, which nowhere appears in the Constitution, was used by Thomas Jefferson in an 1802 letter to a group of Baptists in Danbury, Connecticut, to justify *federal* disengagement in religion while tacitly approving *state* engagement.)[3] Promoters of creationist literature, fearful of the impact of the teaching of evolution upon their children, have sought to sneak their material into a Pennsylvania public school by doctoring the terminology of their manual without substantially altering its content. Still others, fearful of the secularization of schools, have promoted "stealth candidates" with a hidden agenda (say, school prayer). Such subterfuge usually backfires, causing the opposition to retrench even further. Worse, when employed by believers, it dishonors the God they claim to serve by using ungodly means (lying) to advance an allegedly godly end.

Panic displeases God. Fear is a matter of the heart, and our reigning King cares deeply and especially about our hearts, since it is from them that everything else issues (see Matthew 12:33–37; Mark 7:20–23). God cares about *why* we do something at least as much as he cares about *what* we do. Psalm 97 reminds us that, deep down, the fundamental tone of our lives must be joyful confidence in God's sovereign reign, not fear: "The LORD reigns, let the earth *be glad*; let the distant shores *rejoice....Rejoice in the* LORD, you who are righteous, and *praise* his holy name." (Psalm 97:1, 12, emphasis added). When I choose political and social action because I am afraid, even if I can justify that action from Scripture, I am denying God at a deep level. I am acting from unbelief. I am taking his majestic name in vain.

The next time you find yourself driven by fear, or you hear a message that urges you to act out of fear, consider Jesus. Our Lord saw the desperate evils of life far more clearly than we ever will, and yet he never panicked. In *The Waiting Father* Helmut Thielicke wrote:

> What tremendous pressures there must have been within him to drive him to hectic, nervous, explosive activity! He sees...as no one else ever sees, with an infinite and awful nearness, the agony of the dying man, the prisoner's torment, the anguish of the wounded conscience, injustice, terror, dread, and beastliness. He sees and hears and feels all this with the heart of a Savior...Must this not fill every waking hour and rob him of sleep at night? Must he not begin immediately to set the fire burning, to win people, to work out strategic plans...to work...furiously...before the night comes when no man can work? That's what we would imagine the earthly life of the Son of God to be like, if we were to think of him in human terms....But how utterly different was the actual life of Jesus! Though the burden of the whole world lay heavy on his shoulders...he has time to stop and talk to the individual...By being obedient in his little corner of the highly provincial precincts of Nazareth and Bethlehem he allows himself to be fitted into a great mosaic whose master is God...And that...is why peace and not unrest goes out from him. For God's faithfulness already spans the world like a rainbow: he does not need to build it; he needs only to walk beneath it.[4]

Seek God's Glory above Narrow Political Goals

Psalm 97 calls us to exalt a Sovereign whose reigning glory knows no national bounds. And this gives us our second "first principle": our political activism must always serve God's glory worldwide. In other words, model Christian Americans, like their counterparts in Brazil or Korea or wherever, set their hearts first and always on the promotion of God's interests.

Psalm 97 makes this priority vivid. Verse 1 does not read, The Lord reigns; let *Israel* (or America) be glad! Nor does it read, The Lord reigns; let *my family* be glad! These groups must surely join the chorus, but the choir in view is far grander: "Let *the earth* be glad; let the *distant shores* rejoice" (emphasis added). Verses 6 and 7 convey the same idea: "The heavens proclaim his righteousness, and *all peoples* see his glory. *All* who worship images are put to shame, those who boast in idols—worship him, *all* you gods!" (that is, all the different groups of people throughout the world [emphasis added]).

In the classic film *Chariots of Fire* Olympic runner Eric Liddell courageously models this priority. When the Prince of Wales and a number of other powerful figures press him to overturn his conscience-bound decision not to run on the Lord's Day, he politely refuses. A singularly obnoxious figure accuses him of arrogant disloyalty, saying, "In my day it was 'country first, then God.'" Liddell fires back (I paraphrase), "It is you who are arrogant! God made kings. God knows I love my country, but I cannot for the sake of that country do what God forbids."

God's glory, God's victory, the revealing and acknowledgement worldwide of who he is, what he has done, what he is doing, and what he will do—this great purpose drives history. Each nation's saga belongs to this larger one. The history of the United States, so full of God's blessing and goodness, is not for that reason a special history unto itself. It belongs, together with the histories of Peru, Iraq, China, and Senegal, to *his* story.

There is a remarkable moment on the eve of the conquest of Jericho. Joshua meets a strange figure:

[Joshua] looked up and saw a man standing in front of him with a drawn sword in his hand. Joshua went up to him and asked, "Are you for us or for our enemies?"

"Neither," he replied, "but as commander of the army of the LORD I have now come." Then Joshua fell facedown to the ground in reverence, and asked him, "What message does my Lord have for his servant?" (Joshua 5:13–14)

God is neither "for us" nor is he "for our enemies." God is for himself—his own purposes and his own glory. What a moment this was for Joshua. He suddenly realized that he was in the presence of an army far greater than his own. Perhaps even more important he realized that to be the commander of Israel at the gates of Jericho did not automatically put him in the ranks of that army, and he fell to the ground. If this humbling reality was true for Joshua in the days of the theocracy (when God's rule was located in the action of one particular human kingdom) how much more true must it be for us who have no special claim to be God's people simply because we are Americans or belong to a particular political party or are the advocates of a particular plan for making our country a better place. My strong suspicion is that, if we could see what Joshua saw, a great deal of the self-righteous certainty that lies behind our political anger would dissipate, and along with it the anger itself.

America and the Kingdom of God

We can draw at least one implication from this great principle. Many of us have legitimate longings for our country. But our deepest longing must not be that America will be happy or prosperous or safe. Think about foreign policy. Our deepest longing as we think about U.S. activity in the Middle East cannot simply be that America will be protected from terrorism. It must be that our policy there will advance in those countries, if only in small ways, the sorts of things that please and honor Christ—things like justice, mercy, and evangelism. One of the tragedies of modern times is that far too many Muslim people hate Christianity because they equate it with American militarism.

Or think about the American economy. Our deepest longing must not be (as so many hoped in early 2009) that the economic crisis would pass quickly, that people would start spending again, that foreclosures would drop off and employment would rise, and that the "bad guys" (whoever they were—there was, of course, some disagreement about that) would be brought to justice.

We must keep reminding ourselves that a safe and rich America is not necessarily identical with the triumph of God's agenda. Scripture teaches after all that God is glorified not only in his mercies, but also in his judgments. In Romans 1:18–32 Paul describes the social and moral disintegration of an ancient culture—a disintegration disturbingly parallel to what we observe in our own country today—from sexual chaos to greed-driven economic collapse. Paul says that this tragedy did not happen by chance, but was the work of God aimed at making known his holy anger: "The wrath of God is being revealed from heaven against all the godlessness and wickedness of people, who suppress the truth by their wickedness" (Romans 1:18). Like Jeremiah and many of the prophets, the Christian must be prepared to say with tears, "Lord, if you choose to glorify yourself in the failure of our thankless and decadent society (and I hope you do not), then so be it. Honor your name!" Our first love must be God's will and honor, come what may.

We must embrace this difficult truth or we will blind ourselves to things about our country, past and present, Republican and Democrat, that have not pleased God. We must love our country, but we must have lover's quarrels with it (starting with ourselves), for our citizenship is in heaven.

Imagine a world without the United States. An unsettling thought, as unwelcome and as unlikely as the end of their empire would have sounded to Roman citizens at the time of Augustus Caesar. But history and Scripture teach us that nations come and go, and there is no guarantee that America will exist forever. Our duration and stability are in fact anomalies in the saga of human civilization. All human governments will one day fail, and for that reason the Christian sets his deepest hope on the glory of God's reign, not the survival of his country.

Hate Evil

We come now to a third "first principle" for civic life drawn from Psalm 97: Christians must hate evil. Abundant evidence for this principle occurs in the psalm: "Clouds and thick darkness surround him; righteousness and justice are the foundation of his throne....Let those who love the LORD *hate evil*, for he guards the lives of his faithful ones and delivers them from the hand of the wicked" (Psalm 97: 2, 10, emphasis added).

"Clouds and thick darkness" surround God's throne because he is morally unapproachable. That is, he is absolutely holy and we are not. When we read that his throne rests on "righteousness and justice" we learn that every act of his sovereign rule arises from a character and policy that are good and fair. Because of who he is, God will neither act unrighteously nor tolerate anything unrighteous throughout his dominion.

We will consider hating evil more fully in Chapter 9 in our discussion of integrity. At present notice two things about it. First, we are to hate *evil*, not *people*—not even evil people (like those "fiends" across the aisle in Congress!). It is the easiest thing in the world to demonize the opposition—to make an abortion activist or someone promoting tax cuts for the rich the incarnation of all that we hate about what they advocate. We must not do this.

Here is the second thing to note. The mandate to hate evil is for us a double-edged sword. On the one hand it comforts us immeasurably to know that the God who reigns over everything is good. We can know that all that is right and true and lovely will one day be fully vindicated. On the other hand, this truth reminds us that God is on our side *only* insofar as we are on his (remember Joshua's encounter with the angel): "Rejoice in the LORD, *you who are righteous*" (Psalm 97:12, emphasis added).

Who among us can be 100 percent sure, in anything, that God is fully on our side? Even in our most "Christian" moments, we as a nation never enjoyed the special relationship to God that ancient Israel enjoyed. (People have different opinions on how Christian we were once, though it is fair to say that there was a time when a Protestant Christian ethos dominated the culture.) Israel was a theocracy, the kingdom of God located in a human kingdom—something we have never been, despite the rhetoric of some. For this reason we must be wary of the sort of thinking that lifts an event or law out of ancient Israel's civic life and tries to insert it wholesale into the contemporary scene as "God's will for America." A sad example of this was the tendency of some in colonial times to identify the killing of American Indians with the conquest of Canaan.[5]

And even if we were a theocracy, we would still need to be extremely cautious about identifying what is "of America" with what is "of God." After all, for all its privileged status, not even Israel survived the righteous judgment of God when they turned from him. Patient and forgiving for many years, he nevertheless chastened his people, even to the point of exile. If Israel, who enjoyed "most favored nation" status (with God), was punished for sin, can we expect an exemption?

It is a great mistake to think that all the good guys and all the best ideas can be found in one party, usually one's own. If we hate evil we will watch for it close to home. And we will resist it close to home—in the ideas, visions, and strategies of our closest friends and allies (those whose errors we are most apt to overlook). We will never find ourselves buying into everything our party or activist group stands for. And for this reason we will always be a little bit lonely, a little bit out of sync with our fellows, even our fellow believers. This may be hard, but it will keep us humble—and that is always a good thing.

Making It Personal

1. What social issues would you rather not talk about at church, or with Christian friends, or with any friend? Why?

2. Recall a time when you or a friend made a political choice out of panic. Why did you panic? What did you do and what were the results? Why is panic in politics unwise? Why does it displease God?

3. Psalm 97 teaches that God's glory worldwide is the main theme of history. Romans 1 reminds us that God is glorified in judgment just as he is in mercy. Where do you see God's mercy at work in American society? Where do you see his judgment? Talk to God about what you see.

4. The final stanza of Katherine L. Bates' famous song, *America*, reads in part: *"America! America! God mend thine every flaw. Confirm thy soul in self-control, Thy liberty in law."* Scrutinize the political party or activist group that you feel the greatest affinity to. Where does it need mending? What can you do to contribute to that mending? How might your efforts make you lonely?

All who worship images are put to shame, those who boast in idols. (Psalm 97:7)

Do not tremble, do not be afraid. Did I not proclaim this and foretell it long ago? You are my witnesses. Is there any God besides me? No, there is no other Rock; I know not one." All who make idols are nothing, and the things they treasure are worthless. Those who would speak up for them are blind; they are ignorant, to their own shame. Who shapes a god and casts an idol, which can profit nothing? People who do that will be put to shame; such craftsmen are only human beings. Let them all come together and take their stand; they will be brought down to terror and shame. (Isaiah 44:8–11)

Chapter 2

GETTING TO THE HEART
OF THE MATTER

What makes disagreements in the church particularly distressing is that they can be so heated. I have friends whose church exploded over whether or not home schooling was the Lord's preferred way to raise children. How can we be salt and light in our polarized culture when we ourselves cannot agree, or when we cannot disagree amicably? Often the only reason churches don't explode is that Christians of differing politics have already split from each other. Evangelical blacks (who tend to be Democrats) don't as a rule worship with evangelical whites (who have tended to be Republicans—though that is changing). Evangelicals who are closely linked to academia and are more likely to be Democrats tend to drift from evangelicals who are closely linked to business and are more likely to be Republican.[6] Some Christians feel so marginalized by what they see as the church's complicity in mainstream culture—complicity in secularized public education, media violence and promiscuity, family decay, failures in education, intrusive government, and abortion—that they withdraw completely and may fall prey to cultic influence, sometimes even to violent influence.

Why All the Heat?

The sad fact we have been noting is that the church is often as divided, and as angry over our divisions, as is the surrounding culture. Jesus has called us to be the light of the world, and we are often little more than reflections of the divisive darkness that surrounds us. Why do we disagree so much? More important, why do we tend to disagree so heatedly? Why the distrust and name-calling? Why the tendency to withdraw from each other into churches where everyone agrees politically?

One reason, well documented by sociologist James Hunter,[7] is that many Christians have joined the broader culture in the mistaken assumption that public life is the same thing as political life. For this reason we tend to think that the only, or best, way to change the culture is through politics. But politics is intrinsically coercive, using power (rather than persuasion) to bring about change. And forced change tends to turn up the heat in public life; it tends to polarize people, transforming ideas into slogans, discussions into shouting matches, and the opposition into demons. This is the case even when Christians are involved; perhaps more so since Christians tend to feel that they have a mandate from God in their efforts. Christians need to rediscover that "public" is much larger than "political." (Chapters 8 and 9 aim to broaden things out a bit.)

Idolatry Produces the Heat

But why do we seize on solutions, political or otherwise, with such polarizing energy? There is more to the problem than too narrow a definition of public life. The heart of the matter is the heart. Our hearts tend to drift away from their proper center in God. We are, in other words, idolaters, prone to setting our deepest hopes and identities in things other than God. And these false hopes are so fragile that we become angry and afraid when they are threatened, as they so often are by politics. For one reason or another people of differing politics threaten the leaders, strategies, or ways of life that we have come to rely upon too heavily. If, for example, we have built our lifestyles and future plans around a largely deregulated economy, we will tend to become angry (even infuriated) over a political administration that pushes hard for regulation. If on the other hand we have built our lifestyles and future plans around certain governmental social benefits, we may find ourselves growing nervous and angry—even furious—over a political administration that aims to remove or diminish entitlements. (Why, we might well reflect, do we call them "entitlements"?)

The most immediate and perhaps the best thing any of us could do for America is to search our lives and attitudes carefully and repent of our complicity in the idolatries of our time: "*All* who worship images are put to shame, those who boast in idols" (Psalm 97:7, emphasis added).

Think for example of the economic woes of 2008–2009. Many Americans rejoiced to see Bernard Madoff, architect of a $50 billion Ponzi scheme that ruined the lives of many, brought to justice. But how many of us were prepared to admit to our own headlong pursuit of money? Mr. Madoff was a hero as long as he was producing money for us; he became the villain only when he didn't. At the heart of the financial meltdown was what one of my church leaders (himself an executive in one of the firms that came near to collapse) called a "tsunami of debt."[8] Certainly greedy bankers and lazy regulators were key players in this, but vast numbers of us contributed to the problem. How many of us were not drawn into the worship of the "good life" that the world of easy credit offered? How many of us spent far beyond our means simply because we thought we could get away with it?

"Pick your poison" a friend of mine says regarding the idols available to us. Some of us may feel free from the worship of money. But what about other obsessions: celebrity mongering (a recent survey indicated that a distressingly high percentage of teenage girls would rather be "the personal assistant to a famous singer or movie star" than a U. S. Senator or the president of a great university)[9], or sexual addiction (pornography seems to be as much a problem for the church as it is for the rest of the culture). We pour money and energy into sports, into body image, into professional success, and into the acquisition of power. We grow angry at anyone or anything that threatens our freedom to spend as we please or to express ourselves as we please because we have become worshipers of unbridled freedom.

An Idolatrous Vision of America

Consider three common political idols: An idolatrous vision of America, an idolatrous dependence on political power, and an idolatrous pursuit of privacy.

Many of us have a vision of America—which is why we tend to resonate when certain people talk about "The American Dream". Our visions vary of course. They may be deeply religious, drawing their life from America's theological roots in Protestantism. They may be more political, borrowing their energy not so much from *what* the founders believed (there is of course plenty of debate over this), as from the *longing to believe freely* (whatever that belief happens to be). It is not idolatrous to have a dream for America. We become idolators when we permit that dream to become so dominant, so absolute, that there is no room in our hearts for any vision that threatens it (or any person whose vision threatens it). We *must* have vision "A" or vision "B" if we are going to have America. A good sign that we have allowed a dream to turn idolatrous is when we allow a slogan (say, "Make America great again!" or "Pay your fare share in taxes!") to define us and shut down all discussion.

The Idol of Too Much Hope in Politics

Another common idol is undue reliance on government and government leaders. I was deeply moved by the election of Barack Obama in 2008. I did not endorse everything he advocated, but I was nevertheless happily amazed that our country chose to elect an African American—and that such an unprecedented change in power had occurred without violence (a rare thing in world history: John McCain admirably championed that peace when he silenced the bitter voices of his own constituency during his concession speech). When I saw the President-elect's daughters on the victory platform on election night and imagined that they would soon be in the White House, not as guests, but as hosts, I could not help but weep. But in the midst of all the euphoria, I was also troubled by the nearly messianic status that Mr. Obama had come to enjoy. "He is only a man," I kept saying.

We might not rely too heavily on a particular figure, but we might easily do so with respect to a movement. When the Christian Right rose to power in the 1980s, many Christians who had heretofore been inactive politically began to discover that they could affect the national agenda. And with that discovery came a tendency to expect too much of political solutions to the nation's deepest ills.

There is nothing idolatrous about political activism or about advancing skilled politicians whom you feel will push things in a good direction. The idolatry arises when we begin to think that things will be so much better if "we can just get *this law* enacted," or "we can just get *this person* into office and *that person* out of office," or "we can just mandate *this book* for the history curriculum and *that book* for biology." Certainly leaders and policies make some difference—Proverbs speaks of the blessings and curses of good and bad leaders—but not as much as we sometimes think, given our sprawling polity and selfish hearts. How easily (and unfairly) we tend to blame elected officials for the social ills of our time, as if greed, family problems, uneven pay scales, failures in education, and inner-city violence were simply the government's fault. Those in office bear responsibility and their decisions affect our lives to some degree, but such scapegoating, which appears with a vengeance during election years, reflects an unrealistic and idolatrous reliance upon the machinery of government. We often grow to hate certain administrations and figures because we once loved them too much. Just think of the remarkable political reversals in the 2010 and 2018 midterm elections.

Just Leave Me Alone: the Idol of Privacy

If some of us tend to make a god out of public empowerment, others among us tend to make a god out of privacy. Or, perhaps, at different times we tend to make gods out of both. Think about privacy. In certain areas of life we passionately want to be left alone to make our own way. My observation is that we do this whatever end of the political spectrum we occupy. From the left we cry foul whenever religion finds its way into our relationships. ("Religion has no right to impose a particular view of marriage on me!") From the right we cry foul when Uncle Sam finds his way into our wallets. ("Congress has no right to impose such limits on my income!") Those on the left assert the "right" to terminate a pregnancy with as much fervor as those on the right assert the "right" to bear arms. The issues may be different, and may carry different weight, but what awakens the passion in each case is the threat, either perceived or real, to personal freedom. And the passion increases in direct proportion to how fervently we believe that freedom of a certain sort (freedom from constraint) is essential to our lives—the degree, in other words, to which we have permitted it to occupy a godlike place in our hearts.

The worship of privacy may be more of a problem inside the church than we think. Consider the black versus white and business versus academy church divisions we mentioned earlier. We may feel safe and even comfortable "going public" about our politics at church, but that may be only because there is no risk that doing so will invite any challenges. After all, we may have chosen a church where everyone agrees with us (this happens, incidentally, on both the left and the right, and we must examine ourselves before being critical of others about it). Of course, not every church roster is defined by politics. Some churches manage to be big tents politically, but this is often accomplished by avoiding all talk of public responsibility. But isn't this just another way of bowing to the god of privacy?

Consider as another example the disagreements over whether Creationism should have a place in the public school curriculum. Christians find themselves on both sides of the issue (it is too simple, in other words, to see this as an argument between secularists on the one hand and Christians on the other). Some Christians advocate for Creationism because they fear the imposition upon their children of what they see as atheistic philosophy. Other Christians, however, believe that God created through evolution and advocate against Creationism because they fear the imposition upon their children of what they view as bad science. What can add fire to the disagreement is the threat that the opposing party presents to our perceived right to privacy on the matter. No one, whether it is the government or some parental group, should be telling us (and our children) how to do science.

The Idol of Privacy Forgets the Golden Rule

When we make an absolute of privacy, we forget the Golden Rule.[10] This is not only disobedient, which is reason enough to eschew the practice; it also undermines our life as a nation. Let me explain. Many activist believers have sought, for example, to redress the anti-Christian bias in textbooks, or to make public school facilities available after hours for Christian meetings (often with good results), or to pursue litigation in defense of Christian conscience, or to expose the anti-Christian bias in the academy. These are, of course, all worthy undertakings, as far as they go. If Christians do not blow the whistle on anti-Christian bias, who will?

The difficulty, as I see it, is that we often do not go far enough. Our active interest in the freedom of conscience often extends only as far as we have felt *our* rights and freedoms as Christians being threatened. Assuming that you desire prayer in public schools (I realize that Christians differ on the wisdom of doing so at all), would you do so with as much fervor if you lived in Honolulu (where prayer would as likely be to a Hindu deity as to Christ) as you would if you lived in Memphis (which is located in a part of our country heavily populated with Christians)? Perhaps not. Sadly, in our valid concern over the decay of faith in our society, we may find ourselves advocating action that marginalizes the faith of the lonely Jewish kid in the otherwise Christian fourth grade classroom in rural Mississippi.

Do you see the problem? Christians are, or appear to be, religiously self-serving when it comes to their engagement with public life. We can make such an idol of the freedom of our *own* conscience that we become blind to the fact that freedom of *every* conscience is a Christian principle worth fighting for. One need not be a religious relativist to acknowledge this. The Jesus who claimed he was the only way to the Father never forced anyone to believe him. He has no place in his kingdom for coerced disciples, but says instead, "Come to me, all you who are weary and burdened, and I will give you rest" (Matthew 11:28). In a day when so many angrily assert their rights, Christians have a remarkable opportunity to demonstrate a totally different mindset, the mindset of a statesman—one that firmly defends the *non-Christian's* right to believe as he or she does.

I am not suggesting that we cease bringing what we believe into the public discussion. Nor am I suggesting that we cease believing that Jesus Christ is the Lord of all. But I am suggesting that we trust his Lordship enough to obey him when he commands us to love our neighbors as we love ourselves. If we want our voices to be heard in the public debates, we will also want the voices of our Muslim, secular, and atheist neighbors to be heard. We will look for ways to say, in effect, "I think you are dead wrong in what you believe, but I will go to the wall for your freedom to argue for it."[11] We will see as equally worthy of legal consideration the rights of a Caribbean cult to sacrifice chickens in Miami and the rights of a fundamentalist church in rural Ohio to start a school. With a love undergirded by confidence in Christ's ability to promote his kingdom in any setting, we will resist the temptation to be privacy-driven in our religious advocacy, concerned only to defend our turf from our enemies. We will always have an eye on the common good.

If the Golden Rule should apply in the broad world of public life, should it not also apply in the narrower world of church life? Should not Republicans, Democrats, and Independents be able to worship together under the same roof? And should they not be genuinely able to listen to each other, even to disagree vigorously, without blowing the church apart?

Living by the Golden Rule is not easy. It provides no clear-cut answers for how to hold to and advance our deep convictions while also honoring the neighbor who disagrees with us, whether that neighbor is an atheist or a fellow believer. The Golden Rule offers no blueprint for building a safe and godly America. It rather charts a path for us, a path whose end we cannot see, full of difficult turns (complex thinking), steep climbs (the hard work of listening), and sudden descents (humble apologies). But it is the path that Jesus commands, and for that reason we should follow it. Most importantly, the Golden Rule gives us the antidote to the self-protective and community-compromising worship of privacy, for by taking this path we demonstrate that we are worshiping the true God, the God who is big enough to vindicate what is true and real in his own way and in his own time.

The Biggest Idol of All: Ourselves

Of course, we ourselves are the greatest idol of all. Being a citizen is a little like being married. It is living 24/7 with somebody besides yourself (in the case of politics, lots of somebodies). This would be fine if no one except you wanted to be at the center of things. Unfortunately, everyone else is just like you in thinking that his opinion, his candidate, and his strategy for making things better are all the best. This is where the heat in politics comes from most deeply: everybody wants to be king.

Given this analysis we can see where the solution to political heat must begin—and continue. Each of us must surrender the throne he has wrongly assumed. He must surrender it first to God in trusting worship and second to his neighbor in service. Doing these things will not mean that we will no longer have any heartfelt disagreements—even in the church. Nor does it guarantee that if you serve others, they will in turn serve you (people spurned Jesus' love and they may well spurn yours). Nevertheless if you do your part, you will find the heat in you dropping down a notch or two. For your sense that all is well will no longer depend on getting things your way. "Winning" will no longer mean getting your candidate or policy in place; it will mean doing the right thing and leaving the results in God's hands. You will find yourself more able to back down when someone insults you. Winning a school board debate won't be quite as important as it once was. Your ego will no longer be invested in the outcome, and for that reason compromise will be easier. When love begins to replace winning for growing numbers of citizens, life together becomes more tolerable.

Making It Personal

1. One of the chief reasons we become so angry over political differences is that those differences often threaten the idols in our lives—certain ways of thinking or living on which we have grown too dependent. Think of a political policy that you hate and analyze it from the point of view of idolatry. What does this policy threaten in your life? Why are you afraid of losing that thing? Spend some time in prayer asking God to help you abandon the idols that contribute to political heat in your life.

2. The latter part of the chapter describes three idols. The first is an idolatrous vision for America. The second is the tendency to rely too much on politics to bring change. The third is the drive toward privacy. Which of these tends to seduce you the most? Which do you see reflected most vividly in your church? What can you do to reduce the idol's influence over you and your church?

3. In December 1999, the United States Supreme Court agreed to hear a case involving a dispute over whether students at a Texas high school should be permitted to continue their long-standing practice of praying over the stadium public address system just before kickoff at football games. If you were a member of the Supreme Court, how would you rule, particularly in light of the observation in this chapter that "our interest in public life seems to extend only so far as we have felt our rights and freedoms as Christians being threatened"?

4. Discuss the following statement by Don McLeroy, member of the Texas Board of Education, which rules on the content of 48 million textbooks that it buys and distributes annually.

> Textbooks are mostly the product of the liberal establishment, and they're written with the idea that our religion and liberty are in conflict. But Christianity has had a deep impact on our system. The men who wrote the Constitution were Christians who knew the Bible. Our idea of individual rights comes from the Bible. The Western development of the free-market system owes a lot to biblical principles (*New York Times Magazine,* February 14, 2010, 35).

What would it mean for Mr. McLeroy to practice the Golden Rule in his curriculum choices? What would it mean for you to practice the Golden Rule in your response to Mr. McLeroy's statement?

Then the eleven disciples went to Galilee, to the mountain where Jesus had told them to go. When they saw him, they worshiped him; but some doubted. Then Jesus came to them and said, "All authority in heaven and on earth has been given to me. Therefore go and make disciples of all nations, baptizing them in the name of the Father and of the Son and of the Holy Spirit, and teaching them to obey everything I have commanded you. And surely I am with you always, to the very end of the age." (Matthew 28:16–20)

I urge, then, first of all, that petitions, prayers, intercession and thanksgiving be made for all people—for kings and all those in authority, that we may live peaceful and quiet lives in all godliness and holiness. This is good, and pleases God our Savior, who wants all people to be saved and to come to a knowledge of the truth. For there is one God and one mediator between God and mankind, the man Christ Jesus, who gave himself as a ransom for all people. (1 Timothy 2:1–6)

Chapter 3

KEEPING THE CHURCH FOCUSED

Most first-grade classrooms have at least one Tommy the Terrible. We can picture him standing defiantly on his desk. His teacher tells him to sit, but he shakes his head.

> "Tommy, if you do not sit down right away, I will have to come over there and make you sit."

> "You can't make me!" is the reply.

> The teacher walks over to Tommy's desk, picks him up and forces him firmly into his seat.

> "There now, Tommy, you *are* sitting down."

> To which Tommy replies defiantly, "I may be sittin' down on the outside, but I'm standin' up on the inside!"

Societies change most dramatically as people change, one by one, from the inside out, rather than by the imposition of rules and restraints from the outside in or from the top down.[12] Sometimes, of course, those restraints must be imposed. That is why God established government—and the schoolteacher! They are institutions without which people's natural selfishness would reign uncontrollably and make living together impossible. But a greater glory shines, and a better society thrives, when people voluntarily come to bow with joy before the King of kings and this heartfelt allegiance spills over into all of life. Renewed by the indwelling Holy Spirit who writes God's moral law on the heart (see Ezekiel 36:25–28), people need less and less the fear of governmental sanctions to make them live as they should.

Who is responsible for advancing this powerful and strategic solution to society's woes? Clearly, it is the church. After all, if the church does not tell people about the life-changing Christ and does not pray for his presence and gospel to penetrate, who will? This is the church's primary calling, a calling that should caution believers against pouring the church's energies unduly into politics. Whatever we do individually in our efforts to honor the King socially, we must hold the church to Jesus' mandate in Matthew 28.

Diversions and Divisions

Politics in the church can *divert* it from its strategic calling. When the hot social issues of the day drive the church's teaching and activity, they drain it of vital energy that ought to be used elsewhere. I remember working once with a church task force seeking to come up with guidelines on what sorts of political publications should be made available, and how they should be made available, at church. It took months, and we never implemented the unwieldy results of our effort. I completed the undertaking with a strong sense that we would have done better to give our efforts to other matters.

Politics in the church also compromises our primary task by *dividing* people along nonessential lines. This division can take at least two forms. First it divides church people *from each other*. A very imperfect science, politics can be defined as the important but fallible efforts of fallible people to make life in our fallen world better, according to fallible and limited understanding. Because of its imperfections, politics will without fail divide good Christian people from each other as they seek to follow their own consciences, wrestling with the complexity of social and political life. Such differences are not inherently bad; they can reflect the rich diversity of gifts and callings that exist in the body of

Christ. But they can split a church if the church begins to endorse one strategy or calling at the expense of another.

Politics can also divide people *from the church*, a serious problem indeed. Imagine someone visiting your church next Sunday. She has not been to church in years and is coming because of a crisis that has opened her heart to God. Imagine furthermore that she is a staunch Republican, whose parents and grandparents were all involved in Republican politics, and who is herself quite active in local party efforts. Imagine, finally, that as she walks in the door of the church, someone hands her a leaflet that "smells" pro-Democrat. It does not say "vote for so-and-so," but by the way it is formatted, by the issues that it lists, and by the issues it does not list, our visitor knows that Democrats wrote it. What will she do? She may be desperate enough spiritually to stick around and listen to the preacher. On the other hand, she might turn around without a word and leave, saying to herself, *I did not come here to be a Democrat.* Should the church run this risk, not for its sake, but for hers?[13]

Certainly the church does not exist to please people. Jesus said, "I did not come to bring peace, but a sword" (Matthew 10:34). Neither the law of God, which exposes our sin, nor his cross, which offends our self-righteousness, makes people comfortable. But the church must take care that the law and the gospel, and not something else, do the dividing. Our primary concern, concern for the glory of God in the transformation of people through the gospel, should lead us in our corporate life to be a place where people from varied political backgrounds, convinced of varied political strategies, feel socially and politically safe. We must be a place where one's politics does not make him or her a second-class citizen, but rather a place where we can agree to disagree in the spirit of loving dialogue.

Praying Down the Kingdom

In the midst of giving a commencement address, a speaker asked everyone to rise. He then said, "Those of you who do not know the name of your state governor, please sit and remain seated." Some sat down. Then he said, "Those of you who do not know the name of at least one of your state's senators in

Washington, please sit." A larger number took their seats. He continued, "Those of you who do not know the names of *both* your state's senators, please sit." Lots of people sat down. He next asked, "Those of you who do not know the names of your district representatives in your state government, please sit." By that time, all but a handful were off their feet. Then the speaker observed, "Friends, if we do not know the names of these people, how can we be praying for them?"

Perhaps more than any other prophet, Daniel was privileged to see the hand of God behind human history. On one occasion, after a vision had driven him to three weeks of fasting and prayer, a glorious and terrifying figure visited him and said

> "Do not be afraid, Daniel. Since the first day that you set your mind to gain understanding and to humble yourself before your God, your words were heard, and I have come in response to them. But the prince of the Persian kingdom resisted me twenty-one days. Then Michael, one of the chief princes, came to help me, because I was detained there with the king of Persia. Now I have come to explain to you what will happen to your people in the future." (Daniel 10:12–14)

These words remind us that national and international developments are in some mysterious fashion linked to angelic conflict in a world we cannot see. They remind us, furthermore, that when we pray for the nations we lift ourselves into this great conflict.

There is tremendous political power in prayer, especially now that Jesus has ascended "far above all rule and authority, power and dominion." God has "placed all things under his feet and appointed him to be head over everything *for the church*" (Ephesians 1:21–22, emphasis added). This means that we have influence over every government on earth, simply by prayer.

The wonderful thing about political praying is that it is a form of "power politics" open to all. Anyone can do it: the shut-in who can't get out to the polling station, the twelve-year-old who is not old enough to vote, the conscientious citizen who has studied an issue carefully and is still confused about it, the civil servant who is dismayed by the corruption and inefficiency in the department where he works, the soldier on the battlefield, the official in the State Department struggling with how best to respond to an international crisis, the missionary who is being thrown out of an Islamic nation whose government has just turned radical, the national believer who is on trial for her faith, the young black who is pulled over on the highway for racial reasons.

How Do We Pray?

Pray we can, and pray we must. But how should we pray? What comes after "God bless and keep America?" Is this even the right way to pray? Paul gives us helpful counsel in 1 Timothy 2:1–6:

> I urge, then, first of all, that petitions, prayers, intercession and thanksgiving be made for all people—for kings and all those in authority, that we may live peaceful and quiet lives in all godliness and holiness. This is good, and pleases God our Savior, who wants all people to be saved and to come to a knowledge of the truth. For there is one God and one mediator between God and mankind, the man Christ Jesus, who gave himself as a ransom for all people.

Note first off that our praying must be international. "God bless America" is fine, but it is not enough. Paul commands us to intercede and give thanks "for kings and for all those in authority." The world political scene must be on our hearts as we pray. The Bible sets the agenda for prayer, and the evening news fills in the details. It would do our world great good if God's people read the newspaper on their knees!

We should pray "thanksgiving," not simply "requests" and "intercessions." How odd that Paul would counsel thanksgiving in the world he knew, a place of political despotism. But he did, perhaps partly because the fragile church was often wrongfully accused of revolutionary aims and needed for its survival to show its good intentions. But surely Paul had other reasons. He saw government as God's gracious way of controlling the socially destructive impact of sin. He also had the wisdom to see that, for all its imperfections, the Roman rule brought the sort of order and stability that made mission work and evangelism possible. As biblical historian E. J. Goodspeed said,

> "It was the glory of the Roman Empire that it brought peace to a troubled world. Under its sway the regions of Asia Minor and the East enjoyed tranquility and security to an extent and for a length of time unknown before and probably since. It was the 'Pax Romana.'"[14]

Pollsters tell us that Americans are bitter and cynical about their political leaders. One imagines that if any praying gets done at all, its tone is frustrated and content judgmental: "Lord, change that man or get rid of him! Lord, send a firestorm on those self-serving bureaucrats!" We err when we pray this way. It makes the already difficult task of governing in our age even more difficult. Many in government work hard at doing what they genuinely feel best in settings that invariably require compromise and draw flak. Many of the best qualified people never even enter politics, or they leave it, because it is so thankless and difficult. Those who govern us need our encouragement at least as much as our criticism. When we thank God for our leaders, when we call to mind in prayer the good things they do and the efforts they make, we find ourselves behaving more charitably toward them. This change in us fosters a climate in which they find it easier to govern more responsibly. By contrast, negative praying tends to feed the cynicism we are naturally prone to, and cynicism discourages our leaders.

Such a dynamic may be more difficult to envision in national politics than at a local level (we are far more likely to rub shoulders with the members of our district's school board than we are with our state's senators). But I believe that it can happen at any level. Do not underestimate the power of attitude. It cannot be legislated, but it is often more powerful than any law.

According to the apostle the aim of our prayers for world leaders should be "that we may live peaceful and quiet lives in all godliness and holiness." He envisions the maintenance of the kind of national peace and stability that will enable godliness and reverence to flourish openly. And we should desire this, he says, because God "wants all people to be saved" through the "one mediator between God and mankind, the man Christ Jesus." In other words, we should pray earnestly for the nations of the world, that their leaders will establish the sort of peace in which Jesus Christ can be promoted without hindrance. And we must pray this way so that the one true government, God's international kingdom, may be built.

With the collapse of Soviet Russia we rightly rejoiced before God at the end of a godless regime that often oppressed both human freedom generally and Christian proclamation particularly. Where we may have been politically shortsighted and theologically mistaken was in the assumption that this collapse somehow proved that what God really wants everywhere in the world is Western-style democracy and market capitalism. Paul tells us that God longs for "all people…to come to a knowledge of the truth." We must take seriously the possibility that the imposition of America's political and economic traditions wholesale on a different culture (whether it is Russia or Haiti or Iraq or any country) may *not* be God's will, particularly if it causes such political distress as to shut down Christian testimony entirely. And such a shutdown can happen if that testimony is linked to an American "takeover."

How have we and our churches prayed over the conflicts in Syria and Afghanistan? I suspect we have prayed for our soldiers, for their safety, perhaps even for their spiritual well-being and for the effective ministry of military chaplains (civil unrest often brings people face-to-face with the Lord). Certainly it has been right to pray for these things. If we don't pray for our troops, who will?

But Paul, I believe, would have us pray for more. He would have us pray for all the combatants (not only the Americans), for the parents and children caught in the cross fire, for imprisoned insurgents and civilians, and for all the leaders, both political and religious, on every side. He would have us pray for the young men so likely to fall prey to terrorist recruitment in times of uncertainty. He would have us pray for the national Christians in those countries, for the courage and freedom to represent Christ in word and deed. Paul would have us pray that somehow, in the midst of the sorrow, dissembling, violence, and cruelty, people on all sides and in every season and circumstance would meet the merciful God who died and rose to bring to an end the terrible things that we do to each other.

Paul would further have us pray that the Muslim people in those countries not make the mistake of thinking that America somehow represents Christianity. For to make that association would be to identify the God of the gospel with the inevitable imperfections of American soldiers and American foreign policy. To make that association would furthermore suggest that to take an interest in Jesus Christ would be to court western values and culture. It would be to miss the consolation and wonder that the "one Mediator" loves and means to heal every culture.

Think back a bit further to the terrible war that erupted in Yugoslavia after the Soviet collapse. How did you pray then? I suspect you prayed for a quick ending both to the bombing and to Milosevic's ruthless policy of ethnic cleansing. You probably prayed, as I did, for the safety of the pilots, for the safety of noncombatants, and for justice. But did you also pray for the Serbian church? Perhaps the greatest evil of all was the complicity of those who called themselves Christians in the rape and pillage of their Muslim neighbors. How could the loving reign of God's one true Mediator possibly advance under such circumstances? Paul, I am sure, would have had us pray for the Serbian church and its leaders, that by their teaching, example, and prayer, they would subvert the centuries old hatred in the region and exalt the Prince of Peace. He would have had us pray similarly for all believers and their leaders, not just Serbian, but ethnic Albanian and NATO-affiliated. He would have had us pray for political and military leaders (Christian and non-Christian), that by their policies, words, and attitudes they would restrain vengeance and advance the sort of peace that would enable God's people to represent him freely by word and deed.

Prayer: A Corrective to Utopians and Cynics Alike

One of the reasons Christians tend to fight with each other over politics is that we are often secret utopians. We say we trust in Christ, but we really trust in ourselves, or some human solution, to make the world a better place. We keep hoping for and believing in the "silver bullet"—the candidate, the policy, the platform, the Supreme Court configuration—that will fix things. And when we find that someone else's silver bullet differs from ours, we don't trust him anymore—even if he is a fellow believer. Or we keep clinging to the mistaken notion that America is God's chosen nation, positioned to make things right in the world: if we can just get America "right" we will put the world to rights. And when we find someone with a different vision for what it means to get America "right" we demonize him.

Prayer reminds us that utopianism, together with the stridency that often accompanies it, is mistaken. For when we cry "Your kingdom come, your will be done, on earth as it is in heaven," we are appealing to God to do what we cannot do. We are acknowledging the selfishness, blindness, and weakness that drag at us, and will continue to drag at us, until we ourselves are made whole by the coming Lord. We are choosing, in short, to be realists about human solutions. And this realism makes us patient with each other.

To say that prayer makes us realists is not to say that it makes us cynics. To the contrary, it fills us with hope and that hope keeps us engaged. For prayer reminds us not only of what we cannot do, but also of what Christ most certainly will do. And that guaranteed future motivates us to represent him as best we can while we wait for him, even when our efforts are imperfect and seem ineffectual, even when those efforts are not completely in sync with those of other believers.

Someone has said that today's cynic is yesterday's idealist. And this makes sense. For when we begin with the premise that we have in ourselves the full solution to even one small problem, we are bound to be disappointed. And that disappointment will make us either angry or despondent. But the praying Christian begins with a different premise. He looks past himself to the wise God who died and rose to put all things right, and that focus keeps him both humble and hopeful.

Staying on Track

What we have been saying is that we must take care, as God's people, to stay on track. We must protect the church in its high and specific calling, and resist the ever-present temptation to draw it as an institution into the important, but short-term, solutions of politics. We must also pray, humbly, broadly, and continually. Humbly, because we know that we ourselves lack the wisdom and power to fix things ourselves. Broadly, because we know that the God we love is neither an American nor a Korean, neither a capitalist nor a socialist, and he has managed quite ably through centuries of monarchs and despots to save his people, to train them, and to use them in the forward march of his kingdom. Continually, because the deepest battles rage ceaselessy in every heart, including our own, and unless we are praying we will forget this.

Making It Personal

1. Have you ever seen politics divert or divide a church? Describe and analyze what happened. What lessons, if any, did you learn?

2. Take an inventory of your "political" prayer life. Do you know the names of all the public officials who serve you? Do you know their spouses' names? Do you know the issues they are grappling with at the moment? How often and for how long in the past month have you prayed for them? Have you given thanks for their service? How often in the past month have you prayed for a foreign government's officials and policies?

3. Describe your attitude toward politics and politicians. Is it cynical, hopeful, utopian—or something else? Why do you hold your particular attitude? Measure it against what you imagine Jesus' attitude would be. What steps can you take to improve your attitude?

4. Assess the prayer component in your "activism" or in the activism of a friend. Is prayer integrated into the work? If so, is the content of the prayer consistent with the conviction that human solutions are always limited and the hope that Christ will bring the final "fix" to whatever problem is being addressed? What impact does the prayer have upon the tone of the work and the attitudes of the workers? If there is no prayer, what might you do to make it a healthy component of the effort?

5. Carefully read 1 Timothy 2:1–6 and then use it as a springboard to pray for a particular nation or continent. As you do so bear in mind

the following summary of Paul's words: "We should pray earnestly for the nations of the world, that their leaders will establish the sort of peace in which Jesus Christ can be promoted without hindrance. And we must pray this way so that the one God's international kingdom may be built."

Dear friends, I urge you, as foreigners and exiles, to abstain from sinful desires, which wage war against your soul. Live such good lives among the pagans that, though they accuse you of doing wrong, they may see your good deeds and glorify God on the day he visits us. Submit yourselves for the Lord's sake to every human authority: whether to the emperor, as the supreme authority, or to governors, who are sent by him to punish those who do wrong and to commend those who do right. For it is God's will that by doing good you should silence the ignorant talk of foolish people. Live as free people, but do not use your freedom as a cover-up for evil; live as God's slaves. Show proper respect to everyone, love the family of believers, fear God, honor the emperor. (1 Peter 2:11–17)

My prayer is not for them alone. I pray also for those who will believe in me through their message, that all of them may be one, Father, just as you are in me and I am in you. May they also be in us so that the world may believe that you have sent me. I have given them the glory that you gave me, that they may be one as we are one—I in them and you in me—so that they may be brought to complete unity. Then the world will know that you sent me and have loved them even as you have loved me. (John 17:20–23)

Chapter 4

EXEMPLARY AMBASSADORS

I grew up on the north shore of Long Island, spending my summers as a child at a local yacht club where I learned to sail, and where as I got older I found summer employment. One of the most coveted jobs at the club was launch driving. Launch-boys operated the twenty-five-foot inboard yacht tenders that took boaters to and from their vessels. The launches were fun to drive, the job paid well (tips supplemented an already good wage), and the social life was enviable (one could usually get away with ferrying lady friends around the fleet).

The job required a Coast Guard license for which one had to be eighteen and pass an extensive written test. When I was old enough, I applied for the job and to my great delight was accepted, provided I could obtain the license. To my dismay I discovered that before I could even sit for the test I had to document that I had spent at least two hundred hours as a launch-boy trainee—something I had never done. I brought the matter up with my employer, mentioning that I had never heard of any such program at the yacht club. He chuckled and said that, knowing my substantial experience around boats, he would happily testify in writing that I had the required training. This made sense, since the apparent intent of the Coast Guard's stipulation was to assure that launch drivers were "water wise," so I agreed.

That night, however, I couldn't sleep. I desperately wanted the job, but I could not in good conscience be a party to a deliberate deception. After a long struggle, I decided to approach my boss and tell him that I would rather submit to the Coast Guard a summary of my actual boating experience and ask them to accept this in lieu of the training. He couldn't understand why I wanted to do this, remarking that I was clearly experienced enough and that his standard practice had always been to indicate that the training had taken place. Since he kept pressing me for an explanation, I finally took a deep breath and told him that I had to go this route because I was a Christian. Fearful that he might dismiss me altogether as a "holier-than-thou" type sitting in judgment upon his customary practice, I had wanted to avoid this explanation, but he would not let me.

My faith and gratitude soared when he smiled and said, "OK. Good luck." Happily the Coast Guard accepted my experience as valid and I went on to obtain both the license and the job. My boss and I never talked further about the matter, but I hoped in retrospect that Christ used the stand I had taken in his life in some way.

This story dramatizes in a small way the interaction between faith and public life. I could not sleep because I knew that what I wanted and what my boss permitted were not the only standards by which I was to operate. I was Christ's ambassador, called to represent him in this situation, called to submit myself for his sake to every authority.

New Context: Same Principles

Our political experience differs, in some ways dramatically, from the experience of those to whom Peter wrote in the first century AD. We do not live under despotic, or even monarchic, rule. We belong to a representative democracy where we, through our elected officials, are "the king." We live in a tradition that values highly the freedoms of expression, assembly, and worship. And though the church no longer enjoys the cultural dominance it once did, it is not the new and fragile creature it was when the apostle Peter wrote.

Despite the differences between Peter's political world and our own, many deeper truths remain constant. One, noted in the first chapter, is that our God reigns, a profoundly reassuring fact for all who love him and desire to see his justice and righteousness triumph. Another, which we will consider now, is that we, both individually and corporately, have a sociopolitical identity that transcends whatever national or party alignment we have taken on.

Peter calls us "foreigners and exiles" (1 Peter 2:11), aligning us not with the United States or China or a particular political party, but with the kingdom of heaven. If we are Christians, there is a deep sense in which we do not belong here. To use the language of the New English Bible, we are "aliens in a foreign land." We share much in common with Daniel and Esther, Jews who were uprooted from their native surroundings and obliged to live among people whose language, customs, and beliefs differed dramatically from their own. To put the matter positively, we belong most profoundly to Christ, whose reign probes more deeply than any human law can and more widely than the borders of the nation whose passport we carry. Paul wrote, "our citizenship is in heaven" (Philippians 3:20; see also Colossians 1:13 and Hebrews 13:14)—a notion receiving some elaboration in the second century *Letter to Diognetus:* "They [that is, Christians] dwell each in his native land, but only as resident aliens; they carry out all the tasks of a citizen, and endure all the burdens like foreigners; every foreign land is a native land to them, and every native land is a foreign land to them."[15]

Governing Our Hearts

To hold "heavenly" citizenship has searching implications. Human government rules on outward actions—on what we do. But Jesus rules as well on motives and means—on why and how we do what we do. Before we judge another, for example, he bids us examine ourselves: "You hypocrite, first take the plank out of your own eye, and then you will see clearly to remove the speck from your brother's eye" (Matthew 7:5). Jesus knows that we tend to be most critical of people whose failures are most like our own and for that reason he demands that we turn our gaze inward before we turn it outward. Such self-criticism will not necessarily silence us when we turn to evaluate others, but it certainly will humble us. One wonders how much more civil and patient we would be with each other, both outside and inside the church, both with political friends and political foes, if we permitted our King to search us thoroughly.

Jesus has equally searching standards when it comes to "means"—to how we go about advancing whatever agendas we seek to advance. During his earthly ministry he never permitted the ends to justify the means. He refused, for example, to "prove" his Father's love by casting himself from the pinnacle of the temple. Obedience, even the frightful obedience of the cross, was the Father's chosen path to glory, so that was the path he took. With such a Person as our head, we too will frown upon shortcuts, even when we are convinced that the ends are worthy ones. As much as we may despise the philosophy and activism of white supremacists, for example, we will not take the law into our own hands and torch their meeting places. Similarly, we will resist the temptation to "get around" the law forbidding the teaching of creation science in public school the way some sought to in Dover, Pennsylvania. They simply edited their preferred textbook (*Of Pandas and People*) by replacing the words "creation science" with the words "intelligent design" and sought to pass it off as the new, legal, textbook.

Making the Case for the King

Living out our American citizenship in a manner that pleases Jesus depends in large measure upon knowing and believing in our deepest identity. Remembering that we serve a King who loves us enough to have died for us gives us peace and hope regardless of America's condition. Knowing that he searches the heart keeps us honest and humble with one another. Believing that Christ welcomes us as fellow royalty in his court gives us security and a sense of place even if society marginalizes us. Knowing that Jesus' kingdom will never end arms us with patience. Recalling that our Master aims ever to broaden his dominion fires our efforts to be his worthy ambassadors.

The apostle Peter has this last implication particularly in mind: "Live such good lives among the pagans that, though they accuse you of doing wrong, they may see your good deeds and glorify God on the day he visits us. Submit yourselves for the Lord's sake to every human authority….For it is God's will that by doing good you should silence the ignorant talk of foolish people" (1 Peter 2:12–13, 15). Peter commands us to live exemplary public lives, and he does so primarily because he knows that by doing so we will make it difficult or impossible for people to ignore our King.

Holy Freedom

One quality of exemplary public living is what we might call holy freedom. Americans wrangle over freedom with great heat these days. At stake most of the time is a host of private freedoms, freedom to express oneself sexually or artistically or religiously or politically. People tend to frame the debate largely in terms of personal rights: the right of a teacher to carry a Bible to school; the right of a homosexual couple to live together and to share equality under the law with heterosexual couples; the right of filmmakers to depict whatever they choose; the right to produce, distribute, and view pornographic material.

Christians should understand and enjoy freedom. The cross frees us from condemnation under God's law. The Father's love frees us from enslavement to the opinions of people. The Holy Spirit frees us from the bondage to sin. And yet, if we understand the nature of our heavenly citizenship, we will understand that we are not free to do whatever we please. Peter writes, "Live as free people, but do not use your freedom as a cover-up for evil; live as God's slaves" (1 Peter 2:16). My personal freedom is not a freedom from all restraint, but rather a freedom from sin and selfishness. God has set me free to serve him before a watching and often antagonistic world. He has set me free to love people who are not like me and who do not like me—people whose politics differ from mine—even (and especially) Christian people. He has liberated me to "make the case" for his character and ways by the way I live. As Peter puts it, "It is God's will that by doing good you should silence the ignorant talk of foolish people" (1 Peter 2:15).

Squeaky Clean

Do you know that throughout his long career as an evangelist, Billy Graham never traveled alone? Wherever he went he brought with him either his wife or a male traveling companion. Do you know that at the end of every crusade, the Graham organization routinely commissioned an independent audit of all the campaign finances and had the results printed in a major newspaper? These matters are perhaps news to you. What I suspect is not news to you are the stories of other religious leaders' financial or sexual misconduct (one thinks of pedophiles in the Roman Catholic priesthood, or of mega-church pastors caught in extra-marital liaisons, or of televangelist swindlers).

Why do so many more Americans know about fallen leaders' improprieties than about Graham's proprieties? There are perhaps many secondary reasons, but the deepest reason is that the world prefers sin to righteousness. More telling, the world, incited by the devil, wants to avoid the claims of Jesus Christ, and, for this reason, pounces with relish upon anything that will drag down Christ's reputation or make him in some way irrelevant. The apostle Peter knew this (as does the spiritually sensitive citizen of Christ's kingdom) and, therefore, urged us to bend over backward, for the sake of our King and out of love for others, to live public lives that are squeaky clean.

On numerous occasions I have found myself counseling Christian couples who are engaged and living together. Some are sleeping together, others are not (often in the latter case financial reasons are given for the arrangement). Rarely, in either case, has much thought been given to the reputation of Christ and the impact of appearances on a watching world. With alarming frequency professing Christians appear in the news and in everyday life as those who seem unwilling or unable to keep promises. The divorce rate among Christian couples is barely distinguishable from the national rate.

In my experience Christians appear to be as sloppy about paying back loans as anyone. When this happens in the church, the place where we can so easily presume upon one another's generosity (all in the name of trust and love), the results are usually painful and often publicly divisive. Disregarding Paul's command, Christians take each other to court, bringing public shame upon the God who died to make them one (see 1 Corinthians 6:1–11).

My friend John, a Christian business leader, invested in a struggling business in 1992, borrowing significantly to keep it going. It continued to struggle (at one point he found himself writing payroll checks from his own checking account) and finally failed, leaving him in 1994 with several hundred thousand dollars in debt. Newly married and calculating that it would take eight to ten years to pay off what he owed, leaving him at age forty with no savings, John was tempted to file for bankruptcy and walk away. Instead, as he reports it, "my wife and I decided to trust God—to honor and repay the debt." Much to their surprise and encouragement a lucrative and surprising job offer allowed him to repay the debt in less than three years.

The point of this story is not the happy ending (faithful acts do not always yield happy results). It is the account it gives of someone whose faith in Christ gave him the courage and motivation not to break his word with creditors. What governed John in a difficult time was a desire to see Christ honored publicly through his financial integrity. Perhaps the most compelling thing about this story is that I heard it, unsolicited, from one of John's professional associates who reported that he, together with many of John's other colleagues, was deeply impressed that John did not take the easy way out.

Christians who understand their true citizenship are never content merely to be happy in Christ. They aim as well to be above reproach—to live lives that in every part commend their heavenly King. They always deal honestly with people. They keep their promises, small and great. They pay all their bills, including those that are not legally enforceable. And they pay their bills on time. Like my friend John, they are governed by a holy fear at the thought that Jesus Christ might cease to be an issue because of their public behavior. People differ on how deeply the press or Senate ought to be allowed to probe the personal lives of those in public office. Without entering that debate, let me say that every Christian, whether seeking office or not, should be able to stand such a probe.

More Than Just Playing It Safe

Peter says that we should "live such good lives among the pagans that…they may…glorify God on the day he visits us" (1 Peter 2:12). We must aim not only at silencing "foolish people" (1 Peter 2:15), but also at eliciting godly praise from them. This will happen only as we turn from merely avoiding questionable practices and appearances to engaging ourselves in aggressive goodness. Public apathy is no more an option for us than is public scandal.

I remember well the day some law students in my congregation came to me following a sermon on the rights of the unborn. They said, "We agree with you, but what are we to do for pregnant women who cannot or will not raise their children?" Their concern began a process that culminated in a crisis pregnancy center and a number of local shelters for unwed mothers. We must forever be asking, "How can we commend the good, just, and merciful reign of our King if we ourselves are not demonstrating it?"

Exemplary Community

It is not enough for us to be exemplary as individual Christians, we must also be exemplary as communities. The church, in other words, must commend the reign of Jesus by the supernatural quality of its love. Certainly this should be true of the church's outward facing love, but it must be particularly true of its inward facing love.

Leading up to and following the 2004 election, Woodland Hills Church, an evangelical mega-congregation on the outskirts of St. Paul, Minnesota, caught national attention when it lost twenty percent of its membership because pastor Gregory Boyd refused to endorse a Republican agenda. He refused to do this not because he was pro-choice or because he sought to defend gay marriage (he was conservative on these issues). He did it because of his understanding of the role of the church. "When the church wins the culture wars, it inevitably loses," Mr. Boyd preached. "When it conquers the world, it becomes the world. When you put your trust in the sword, you lose the cross" (Laurie Goodstein, *New York Times,* June 30, 2006). Despite the fact that Rev. Boyd took six sermons to explain himself, one thousand members of the congregation left.

Why, we must ask, did this exodus happen? I suspect that if the thousand had been polled regarding their view of Christ, the centrality of the cross, and the doctrine of the Trinity, they would have been on the same page as the four thousand who stayed. This means that it had to be something else—a lesser thing from God's perspective—that led to the division. No doubt the reasons from person to person varied in the details, but the fact remains that twenty percent of a church "walked" because of politics—despite the fact that Jesus prays that we "may be one" as he and his Father are one, so that "the world will know that you sent me and have loved them even as you have loved me" (John 17:22, 23).

Much is at stake here. If the crucified and risen Messiah cannot hold Democrats and Republicans together under the same roof, if he cannot enable them to work through their differences, then he is not much of a Savior—he certainly is not the Messiah of the world. Stories like Woodland Hills "prove" that in the final analysis, we are a social organization just like any other social organization—united by the same sort of bonds that unite other human groups, and apt to dissolve for the same reasons that other human groups dissolve.

This is more than unfortunate. It is disobedient, a betrayal of our Savior, the cause to which he has called us, and the purpose for which he died. It proves that we have allowed our vision for America to capture our hearts more deeply than God's vision for us as his ambassadors. And the effect is to compromise the power of our testimony to the world.

On the Edge of Eternity

As I write, my office and house are in disarray. Furniture long in need of reupholstering is at the shop; our den floor (long in need of refinishing) is bare and awaiting a second coat of polyurethane; files long overdue for purging are being purged. We have undertaken all these things at once because in four weeks we will be moving. The deadline has focused us remarkably.

None of us knows precisely when we will be "moving" to glory. What we do know is that the move is certain, it may happen at any moment, and, when it does, the Lord will make all things right. These certainties give focus to our daily living. The apostle Peter certainly believed these things and counseled his readers, many of whom were suffering in their role as ambassadors, to draw their hope from them. He reminded them of the day when their accusers would "see [their] good deeds and glorify God" (1 Peter 2:12).

This may sound morbid or vindictive, and indeed it can be. But it was neither morbid nor vindictive for Peter and the apostles, whose writings resound with rejoicing and love. For them the nearness of the end gave fullness and hope to the present. It made every moment and every personal encounter (even with those who hated them) important. Knowing that the good for which I am working will certainly be vindicated gives me hope. And knowing that vindication may come before the day is over, despite appearances, energizes that hope remarkably. Knowing the person I am speaking with may at any moment meet God makes me eager to commend God's holy love by my behavior. Knowing that the church will one day be revealed in the fullness of her majestic glory and unity makes me eager not to see her dividing over secondary issues—like the best way to see marriages made stronger in America. James Packer invites us to learn from the Puritans here:

> Dr. Johnson is credited with the remark that when a man knows that he is going to be hanged in a fortnight it concentrates his mind wonderfully, and in the same way the Puritans' awareness that in the midst of life we are in death…gave them a deep seriousness, calm yet passionate, with regard to the business of living that Christians in today's opulent, mollycoddled, earthbound Western world rarely manage to match. Few of us, I think, live daily on the edge of eternity in the conscious way that the Puritans did, and we lose out as a result. For the extraordinary vivacity, even hilarity (yes, hilarity; you will find it in the sources), with which the Puritans lived stemmed, I believe, from the unflinching, matter-of-fact realism with which they prepared themselves for death, so as always to be found, as it were, packed up and ready to go. Reckoning with death brought appreciation of each day's continued life, and the knowledge that God would eventually decide, without consulting them, when their work on earth was done brought energy for the work itself while they were still being given time to get on with it.[16]

We are ambassadors of Christ, and, like any ambassador, we may at any moment be summoned home to give an account of what is going on at our post.

Though looming judgment ought not to terrify us, since we are saved by grace rather than works, it should change us. It should make us ask with each new morning, "Lord, knowing that *today* may be the last day of my life—perhaps even of the world—how shall I make things more suitable for your coming?" It should make us as a church ask each Sunday as we gather, "Knowing that *today* may be the last day of every social organization on earth except the church— including both the ACLU and the NRA, including both NRL and NARAL— how shall we keep those groups from driving and dividing us?" Knowing that *today* might be *the* day should inspire us to continue in well-doing, and it should inspire us to look for ways to understand and work with each other, even when we deeply disagree. Jesus died to make us *both* good and one, and he may be on hand in five minutes to complete what he has started.

Love for Our Neighbor

Zeal for the coming Christ and love for people go together. Our practice of public goodness aims not to put people down but to win people to him before it is too late. What our culture needs these days is a vibrant, plausible, winsome Christianity. Intellectual and philosophical arguments are important and good, but they cannot stand alone. They must come from lives of people who have evidently been changed for the better by the God they profess. Do we love people enough, we must ask, to showcase—by how we talk, how we do business, how we do politics, how we treat people, and how we as Christians get along with each other—something of the goodness, justice, loyalty, beauty, and love of our true home?

Why does Christ get such bad press in our day? Why does he often get no press at all? And why, therefore, is the world so ill prepared for the Day of the Lord? Could it be, at least in part, because we are not the winsome ambassadors we should be?

Making It Personal

1. Read 1 Peter 2:11–17 (found at the head of the chapter). Why, according to the passage, should we live exemplary lives? How can our freedom as believers be a "cover-up for evil"? Have you ever seen such a cover-up? How, practically speaking, do we "show proper respect to everyone"? How does the proper respect due a child differ from what is due a parent, or a spouse, or a traffic cop?

2. Recall a situation in which the call to be Christ's ambassador in a public way weighed heavily on your conscience. What did you do about it?

3. Read over the following portion of the ancient *Letter to Diognetus*: "They [that is, Christians] dwell each in his native land, but only as resident aliens; they carry out all the tasks of a citizen, and endure all the burdens like foreigners; every foreign land is a native land to them, and every native land is a foreign land to them." Put into your own words the tension described here. Do you feel that tension? If so, why? If not, why not?

4. Read the book of Daniel or the book of Esther. How were the experiences of these people like our own? What lessons can we learn from them about how to live as a "resident alien" today?

5. How does one live a life that is "squeaky-clean" (above reproach at work, in one's financial dealings and in one's sexual behavior) without being or appearing to be an unapproachable prude or a frightful bore?

6. Why is it not sufficient that our individual lives are exemplary? Why is harmony in the church equally significant? Read Ephesians 2 and 4. How well is your church expressing Christian unity? Does it maintain unity by never talking about potentially divisive social and political issues? By only welcoming one sort of politically affiliated person? How could things improve?

7. How often do you think about your own mortality and that of the people you meet? What would it take for you to recover a sense of urgency about drawing people toward Christ by living a life of positive goodness?

They sent some of the Pharisees and Herodians to Jesus to catch him in his words. They came to him and said, "Teacher, we know that you are a man of integrity. You aren't swayed by others, because you pay no attention to who they are; but you teach the way of God in accordance with the truth. Is it right to pay the imperial tax to Caesar or not? Should we pay or shouldn't we?"

But Jesus knew their hypocrisy. "Why are you trying to trap me?" he asked. "Bring me a denarius and let me look at it." They brought the coin, and he asked them, "Whose image is this? And whose inscription?"

"Caesar's," they replied.

Then Jesus said to them, "Give back to Caesar what is Caesar's and to God what is God's." And they were amazed at him. (Mark 12:13–17)

Chapter 5

TWO KINGDOMS

A number of years ago, we stripped the sanctuary of our church so that we could install a new carpet. One item we removed for the renovation was the American flag that for years had occupied a prominent place on the platform just behind the pulpit. When it came time to put everything back, my associate and I decided not to restore the flag to its customary spot, but to set it up in the back of the church. We reasoned that since Christ is Lord of all the nations, and not simply the United States, it did not make sense to make the symbol of our country quite so prominent in the place where we routinely gather to exalt him. We felt the force of this argument rather strongly since our worship service routinely drew international students from the nearby university. We reasoned further that since America ought to join the nations in submitting to Christ, the flag that symbolizes our land should "sit in the pews" with the rest of the congregation. Its traditional location next to the pulpit suggested too strong a link between what America says and what God says. It ran contrary to the sentiment expressed in the second stanza of "America the Beautiful": "America, America! God mend thine ev'ry flaw, confirm thy soul in self-control, Thy liberty in law."

Despite our careful reasoning, our many reassurances that we loved our country, and our plan to leave the flag in the sanctuary (simply in another location), our decision drew a tremendous amount of heat from some people.

Lots of Questions

I will leave you to guess what we eventually did with the flag. For the moment, let me try to answer "Why all the heat?" The answer is that we do not always find it easy to "give back to Caesar what is Caesar's and to God what is God's" (Mark 12:17). By those revolutionary words Jesus taught us to distinguish a dual citizenship, but he did not make clear precisely how to do it. Christians can disagree strongly on what our double allegiance looks like in practice.

If you had been eligible would you have fought in World War II? In Vietnam? In Desert Storm? In the Iraq War? In Afghanistan? Would you have flown bombing runs over Serbia during NATO's air war with that nation? Or over Libya during NATO's police action against Colonel Gadhafi's brutal regime? Chances are, your answers to these questions are not uniform. Sorting out our dual allegiance to God and to Uncle Sam is not simple.

If Christ is Lord of all, what right does Uncle Sam have to require any allegiance of me? Is it really possible to be both a sold-out Christian and a loyal American? And if some allegiance is due to my country, what are its limits? When, if ever, and how should I disobey the law or a representative of the government? How do I talk with fellow believers about "hot issues" without dividing or diverting the church? These are some of the questions we will try to address in the pages ahead.

Jesus Talks Politics

We should first take a closer look at Jesus' words in Mark 12:17, quoted above. In their setting they are quite remarkable. A brilliant parry of his enemies' efforts to trap him, they also offer profound and revolutionary insight into the believer's relationship to government. Before considering the words themselves, we should note simply that Jesus openly talked about tough political issues. Paying taxes to Caesar infuriated some people. The Jews of that time lived in Palestine under a foreign government, parallel in some ways to the French during the German occupation in World War II (or to Afghans living with foreign soldiers in their streets—a less comfortable parallel for

Americans to contemplate). Though cryptic and influenced by the ulterior motives of his opponents, Jesus' comments nevertheless took seriously the practical social problem presented by the question.

Jesus' readiness to talk politics reminds us of his claim to rule the whole of life. He means to reign not merely over our private worlds—the world of family, close friends, personal devotions, and so on—but our entire world, including our political life. Notice that Jesus answers the political question with a command, not just a suggestion: "Give back to Caesar what is Caesar's and to God what is God's." Our Lord requires appropriate allegiances of us. He does not permit us to treat political questions as non-questions, matters that we can take or leave because they are irrelevant to our obligation to him.

Two Kingdoms

According to Jesus, our obligation begins with the necessity of making a mental distinction between God's government and human government (we cannot render to each its due until we have done this). We make this distinction readily in our day, at least in theory. Beneficiaries of the remarkable political philosophy summarized by the First Amendment, we tend to scorn the Crusades, Oliver Cromwell's protectorate, and some modern Islamic states, all of which sought or seek to advance religion by force. I remember laughing grimly when I first heard of the "christianized" Roman army's practice of marching its conquests in chains through a river and pronouncing them baptized Christians (thereby subject to the emperor) as a result. Such behavior fails to distinguish as our Lord does here; it equates a political undertaking with a religious one.

What is perhaps obvious to us was quite radical in Jesus' day, certainly for a Jew. Israel under Moses, Joshua, David, and the kings that followed him had been theocratic. God's doings in the world had found unique and particular expression in the undertakings of their nation. They dispossessed, and in some cases wiped out, people who did not share their beliefs, often at God's command. Though pious Jews knew that Yahweh was not just another local deity confined to Jerusalem,[17] they nevertheless believed that the Lord of heaven and earth had set his name in that city, and that when David went off to war, so did the Lord.

The Jews of Jesus' day knew well the stories of Egypt's drowning in the Red Sea, of the conquest of Canaan, of Gideon's and Samson's triumphs over the Midianites and the Philistines, and of David's and Solomon's expansive reigns. Many had drawn inspiration from the story of the Lord's triumph in the desperate siege of Jerusalem during Jehoshaphat's reign: "Do not be afraid or discouraged because of this vast army. For the battle is not yours but God's" (2 Chronicles 20:15). Many longed for a revived theocracy, savoring the memory of the Maccabean revolt against foreign apostasy and oppression in the second century B. C. For many, Caesar was another Antiochus Epiphanes (the pagan and murderous oppressor against whom Judas Maccabeus led his revolt), Rome was the kingdom of darkness, and Jesus was the new liberator. They anticipated political Israel in ascendancy with Jesus the Son of David on the throne.

And then Jesus astounded them by saying they should pay Caesar his due. (The NEB captures the strong Greek verb well: "They heard him with astonishment.") Jesus implied here that the Jews actually owed Caesar something, a shocking statement under the circumstances.

A Radically New Pattern

There is much more than shock value in these words. Jesus ushers in a whole new understanding of the believer's political life. In distinguishing between the two governments, he effectively calls us to stop thinking theocratically. We must no longer build or envision a particular earthly society as the location of God's exclusive interest and blessing. Jesus meant it when he told Pilate "My kingdom is not of this world" (John 18:36).

Our Lord's wise words, furthermore, provide us with a marvelous balance as we seek to relate to our government. On the one hand, he teaches us that it is possible to be a sold-out Christian *and* a good American. Not to give our country its due is in fact to disobey Jesus, who commanded us to do that very thing. On the other hand, Jesus also taught that our ultimate allegiance cannot go to the United States, since that would be to deprive God of his due: "Those words…gave to the civil power, under the protection of conscience, a sacredness it had never enjoyed and bounds it had never acknowledged, and they were the repudiation of absolutism and the inauguration of freedom."[18]

Sorting Out the Double Allegiance

Acknowledging both "Caesar" and God does not determine for us precisely what we owe to each. How do we sort out our dual citizenship?

Let's return to the problem of the flag in the sanctuary. Why did some people respond with so much emotion to our decision to move the flag? I know that at least part of the reaction grew from personal history. Every complainer had served honorably or had been married to someone who served honorably in the armed forces. Some had seen combat in World War II. Moving the flag suggested to them that we cared little for the great freedoms we enjoy as Americans and the great cost at which those freedoms have been secured. My associate and I quickly realized that whatever we did, we needed to respect the sacrifice and patriotism of many in our congregation.

The issues raised by the flag episode, however, go beyond personal feelings. Biblical scholars have long debated what Scripture teaches about the practical relationship between the two kingdoms. Some (called "positivists") argue that since God ordains every government, submitting to our government *is* submitting to God. They justify their view by appealing to Romans 13:1–2:

> "Let everyone be subject to the governing authorities, for there is no authority except that which God has established. The authorities that exist have been established by God. Consequently, whoever rebels against the authority is rebelling against what God has instituted, and those who do so will bring judgment on themselves."

We honor God by honoring our country, since he sovereignly raised it up.

Martin Luther championed the positivist view when he strongly opposed the "murderous hordes of peasants"[19] who revolted against their overlords in the peasants' revolts of 1524 and 1525. American flags next to the pulpit in American churches might make sense given this understanding, as might serving in the armed forces, regardless of the conflict in view.

Positivists run into some practical difficulty when facing political injustice. They cannot, for example, easily justify the revolution that brought the United States into existence. Our Declaration of Independence argues that there are times "in the course of human events [when] it becomes necessary" to take up arms against a tyrannical government. On what grounds, it might be argued, is it *ever* necessary (or justifiable) to resist a government that God has sovereignly established. Even if it could be proven that British colonial rule in the 1770s was more oppressive than that of imperial Rome in Paul's day, the simple fact remains that, according to Romans 13, God set King George on the throne. To buck George, it would seem, is to buck God—a course of action very difficult to justify. Positivists, in short, say, "Do nothing," when our hearts say, "Do something!"

As it turns out, our intuitive and practical critique of the positivist approach has strong theological grounds. We claim to believe in a God who is good and just. How, it is argued, can we claim to be his followers if we refuse to take up arms against the Hitlers of this world? Those who hold this view (often called "normativists") also appeal to Romans 13, where we read, "Rulers hold no terror for those who do right, but for those who do wrong" (Romans 13:3). They argue that such words describe a government as it *should* be according to God's design. When the government fails to live up to its God-given responsibility then it may legitimately be resisted, from within (by revolution) and from without (by war). Augustine, among others, speaks of "just war" from this perspective:

> Peace is the aim of wars, with all their hardships…Now when the victory goes to those who were fighting for the juster cause, can anyone doubt that the victory is a matter for rejoicing and the resulting peace is something to be desired? These things are good and undoubtedly they are gifts of God. But if the higher goods are neglected, which belong to the City on high, where victory will be serene in the enjoyment of eternal and perfect peace—if these

goods are neglected and those other goods are so desired as to be the only goods, or are loved more than the goods which are believed to be higher, the inevitable consequence is fresh misery, and an increase of the wretchedness already there.[20]

Though the peace achieved when justice triumphs must never divert our hope from the peace that Christ alone will bring the nations (the point Augustine makes at the end of his statement), the lesser peace is nonetheless cause for legitimate rejoicing. For this reason, bearing arms to secure that lesser peace is justifiable, a necessary evil in a world that is not yet fully redeemed. The propriety of displaying an American flag next to the pulpit might, given this approach, vary depending upon America's social policies at the time. Perhaps the best place would be in the back of the church.

A difficulty with the normativist view is that it does not precisely define when "Caesar" steps out of bounds, thus opening the door to violent attacks on government from any "liberator" who decides for whatever reason to appoint himself to the task. Another difficulty with the normativist view is that it promotes the troubling notion of a "necessary evil" –say killing people in a so-called "just war." But how can the Christian disciple ever justify evil, however "necessary"? Doesn't Christ call him away from *all* evil?[21]

There remains at least one other approach. John Yoder, a modern promoter of this view, calls us to "revolutionary subordination"[22] on the basis of the teaching and example of Jesus. In Yoder's understanding, America (like every government) exists with God's permission, and we must therefore respect it. But our country's days are numbered, since at the cross Jesus demonstrated and instituted a radically new system of governance, based not upon power but upon love. We submit to our government, but we do so in love, not fear, knowing that it is only a matter of time before that old order will disappear. Thus we are free, even as we submit, for our hearts and hopes are not tied to human government at all. Yoder says, "The subordinate person becomes a free ethical agent when he voluntarily accedes to his subordination in the power of Christ instead of bowing to it either fatalistically or resentfully."[23]

Those who hold this third view (often called pacifists) permit political resistance—even encourage it in the face of oppression. But that resistance must be nonviolent, since to resist violently compromises Christ's ethic. For the same reason, pacifists refuse to bear arms. Menno Simons, a sixteenth-century priest after whom the Mennonites take their name, wrote

> The regenerated do not go to war, nor engage in strife. They are the children of peace who have beaten their swords into plowshares and their spears into pruning hooks, and know of no war…Since we are to be conformed to the image of Christ, how can we then fight our enemies with the sword?…Spears and swords of iron we leave to those who, alas, consider human blood and swine's blood of well-nigh equal value.[24]

American pacifists might well be reluctant to display an American flag next to the pulpit, since that too readily equates a human government with Christ's radically different administration, and they would not bear arms. They might even want the flag removed entirely.

In my view the normative position makes the best sense of both Scripture and life. According to the New Testament we live in the "last days," the season in the history of redemption bordered by the first and second comings of Christ. This means that we are caught in the tension between what theologians have called the "already" and the "not yet." On the one hand, Christ has died, has risen, and is now ruling at the right hand of God. He has triumphed over the kingdoms of this world, both seen and unseen, and it is only a matter of time before the ethic of love and goodness will define every part of human social life, both private and public. On the other hand, we await Christ's return. Until that day, and even on that day, he will restrain and punish human cruelty and oppression, by force if necessary.

Living with Two Ethics

Living as we do between Christ's two advents, we must find a way to live with both ethics at once—with both the Sermon on the Mount and with Romans

13. One possible way of doing this is by distinguishing between our behavior as individuals and our behavior as agents of our government.

Two scenes from the film *Saving Private Ryan* illustrate the distinction.[25] The first occurs on D-Day at the moment when the American soldiers finally gain mastery of a German bunker from which the enemy has been slaughtering their fellows all day. The German soldiers emerge, hands in the air signifying their surrender, and they are shot dead at point-blank range. Up until the point of the German surrender, the American soldiers were shooting to kill or at least to put the German defenders out of action. In so doing they were serving as agents of the state in an international "police action" whose purpose was to bring to an end an evil regime. They were, in short, legitimately using force as a kind of necessary evil (or, better, as a form of tough love) to overthrow a greater evil. At the moment of the German surrender, however, a second ethic (or, perhaps better, a more merciful love) should have kicked in. A Christian soldier covering the surrendering Germans might well have been tempted to avenge the death of his comrades, but for Christ's sake he should have resisted that temptation and sought to protect and meet the needs of the POWs.

In the second scene an American platoon encounters a German machine-gun nest in a field. They storm the nest and capture it, leaving all but one German soldier dead. In the process, their medic (a noncombatant) is killed by the surviving German. Angry at their commander for having ordered the attack in the first place (they could have simply gone around the field), and murderous toward the captured German who has just killed their friend, the Americans make their captive dig his own grave, fully intending to kill him. The mutinous standoff that ensues between the officer (who will not allow the killing) and his men nearly issues in more bloodshed. In this case the behavior of the commander vividly illustrates the dual ethic we have been considering. First, he orders the attack on the German machine gunners, an order that legitimately involves killing. But then, after the surrender, he refuses to allow himself or his men to give in to personal vengeance—he acts, in other words, by the ethics of the kingdom to come.

It must be extremely difficult to live by these two standards, especially in a battle situation. It must at times appear absurd. But that does not make it wrong to try. A Christian police officer may legitimately use his gun to keep a violent teenager from shooting his partner. But once he subdues the teenager, he may not in good conscience harm the teen, even if the teen has killed his partner in the process of being subdued. The difficulty and seeming absurdity in situations like this may distress us,[26] but they should not surprise us. Our world is still fallen. Christ has come: he is working through us to make things better, but we must await his return before all is made right.

A Love Too Broad to Settle in One Place

Our Lord's distinction between the two kingdoms does more than point us in a helpful direction as we try to sort out our allegiance to our government. It also fans our hopes by pointing toward his great redemptive plan for the nations of the world. Remember that in differentiating between Caesar and God, Jesus was disassembling the theocracy. No longer was God going to associate his reign with one particular people. And this is so not because God no longer has a saving interest in any nation, but because he has a saving interest in every nation. Jesus knew that with his coming God was ushering in a whole new scenario for the world. Israel was to lose her "monopoly" on God, not because God did not love Israel, but because he chose not to love Israel *only*. The kingdom Jesus announced in his preaching and inaugurated on Pentecost counts as its citizens people living all around the world.

Billy Graham came to Long Island for a crusade in the 1990s. The internationality of the New York metropolitan region found vivid expression in those who gathered. I remember with delight a huge Korean choir singing "Amazing Grace" in their native tongue, Steve Green singing a gospel tune in Spanish, and a Chinese friend doing spontaneous translation for a large delegation of Mandarin speakers. Most moving of all were the interpreters, who with exquisite grace of movement brought all that was said and sung into the silent world of the deaf who had come to "hear." Observing all this,

I thought with great joy, *Now this is the kingdom of God, the reign of the King of kings breaking in upon every tribe and nation!*

Surely God has blessed America and continues to do so. Surely many Christians and much Christian thinking have influenced us for the good down through the years. But to confuse these facts with the notion that we are in some special sense God's country is to forget Jesus' distinction and to shrink God's gracious plans. God's love is simply too great to be bottled up in one language or in one location or in one people.

Reining in Our Political Expectations

Distinguishing between the two kingdoms helps keep us politically realistic and sane. For if we give God his due, then no human governor or government will be worthy of either our highest hopes or of our unthinking allegiance. We all suffer in some way from the utopian impulse, the idolatrous voice (noted earlier) that urges us to lean on people to accomplish more than they are capable of. Sometimes the impulse proves ironic, even silly, as when our euphoria over the election of our favorite candidate turns to bitterness in six months. Both reactions are driven by unrealistic expectations.

At other times abandonment to the utopian impulse yields unspeakable misery, as the twentieth century amply illustrated. The Russian people and later the German people gave way to the impulse to allow the political promises of Marxism and fascism to obscure their vision, thus unleashing a spate of horrific "experiments" in social engineering worldwide.

Christian citizens know that God will not share his glory with another (see Isaiah 42:8) and that the key to social transformation must therefore lie outside human effort. We realize that the problems of drugs in the city, violence in the home, greed in the marketplace, racism in the company, and chaos in the classroom will not be solved simply by spending more money or implementing new programs. Our realism makes us patient with the imperfections of government and its agents (the president, the mayor, the police), knowing that the power for deep societal change does not come from that quarter. We criticize less and pray more, not as an alternative to working as best we can for a better society, but as an expression of our reliance, as we work, on the Ruler of all.

We have already noted that today's cynic is yesterday's idealist. Christian citizens do not give way to political cynicism—or to the apathy that often accompanies it—because from the start we have been realists. We carry on the best we can to make a fallen world better, but we never forget that we await the kingdom of God, a kingdom that Christ taught us never to equate with something we can produce. Caesar and God are not the same.

Making It Personal

1. Consider the American flag story at the opening of the chapter. Where would you have placed the flag and why?

2. Read Lord Acton's interpretation of Jesus' famous statement, "Give back to Caesar what is Caesar's and to God what is God's": "Those words... gave to the civil power, under the protection of conscience, a sacredness it had never enjoyed and bounds it had never acknowledged, and they were the repudiation of absolutism and the inauguration of freedom." Use your own language to describe the balance that Acton believes Jesus' words bring to the way we should order our political life. Discuss modern examples of the "protection of conscience" and of the absence of such protection. How, practically, do we treat the role of a police officer (or of a senator) as sacred while at the same time putting boundaries around that role?

3. Using the positivist, normativist, and pacifist distinctions found in this chapter, compare how you would have behaved toward Hitler if you were a German citizen in 1939 with how you would have behaved toward King George if you were an American colonist in 1776. Why the difference, if any?

4. Read Matthew 5–7 (the Sermon on the Mount) and Romans 13:1–7 (where Paul speaks of the government justly wielding its power). How, taken together, do these texts help us sort out our double allegiance to both God and our government?

5. The end of the theocracy means that God does not give special status to any particular nation or culture. This means, among other things, that we must temper our nationalism with a genuine love for and interest in all peoples. Reflect on the following questions: Do we have any friends from other nations and cultures? If not, what might we do to cultivate some? Do we need to admit to racial prejudice? Do we often make snap judgments about people solely on the basis of their skin color, language, or accent? Do we count as inferior, or unworthy of humanitarian aid, the citizens of countries that are unfriendly to the United States? Do we resent or fear refugees seeking asylum in the United States?

Let everyone be subject to the governing authorities, for there is no authority except that which God has established. The authorities that exist have been established by God. Consequently, whoever rebels against the authority is rebelling against what God has instituted, and those who do so will bring judgment on themselves. For rulers hold no terror for those who do right, but for those who do wrong. Do you want to be free from fear of the one in authority? Then do what is right and you will be commended. For the one in authority is God's servant for your good. But if you do wrong, be afraid, for rulers do not bear the sword for no reason. They are God's servants, agents of wrath to bring punishment on the wrongdoer. Therefore, it is necessary to submit to the authorities, not only because of possible punishment but also as a matter of conscience. This is also why you pay taxes, for the authorities are God's servants, who give their full time to governing. Give to everyone what you owe them: If you owe taxes, pay taxes; if revenue, then revenue; if respect, then respect; if honor, then honor. (Romans 13:1–7)

Submit yourselves for the Lord's sake to every human authority....Show proper respect to everyone, love the family of believers, fear God, honor the emperor. (1 Peter 2:13, 17)

Chapter 6

GIVING CAESAR HIS DUE

Speaking at Gettysburg in November of 1863, Abraham Lincoln urged his hearers to dedicate themselves "to the great task remaining before us— that from these honored dead we take increased devotion to that cause for which they gave the last full measure of devotion." By "last full measure of devotion" he meant the sacrifice of their lives, a sacrifice made "that [their] nation might live," and that "this nation, under God, shall have a new birth of freedom—and that government of the people, by the people, and for the people, shall not perish from the earth."

Lincoln evidently believed that preserving the union and ending slavery in that union were causes worth dying for. Robert E. Lee, a man whose faith in Christ was perhaps deeper than Lincoln's, felt that the preservation of Virginia's freedom from northern intrusion was also a cause worth dying for. Their aims certainly clashed, but these two great leaders agreed that serving God and serving one's country, even to the point of death, may be compatible. They agreed, in other words, with Augustine's notion of just war.

Though I may never be asked to die for my country, giving "Caesar" his due may legitimately call me to make many other sacrifices, some of which we will consider in this chapter.

Charles D. Drew

Separate Worlds?

First, we need to look again at Jesus' command in its first-century context, together with Paul's and Peter's elaborations of it. Jesus' endorsement of Caesar must certainly have shocked many of his countrymen. Caesar was a foreign oppressor. Somewhat wiser in his tolerance of Judaism than Antiochus Epiphanes, the pagan and murderous oppressor against whom Judas Maccabeus led his revolt, he nevertheless ruled as a pagan Gentile in the land that God had given to Abraham. To make matters worse, he counted himself divine. "Tiberius Caesar Augustus, Son of the Divine Augustus" appeared on the coin that Jesus had brought to him when confronted with the question about paying taxes (see Mark 12:13–17).

We are rightly astounded that Jesus should have tolerated such an inscription, not to mention acquiescing in its author's demand for money. And yet Jesus did. Why? Did our Lord believe that God rules one area of life (the religious and spiritual one) while human beings rule another (the political and social one)? Did Jesus, in other words, see life as made up of at least two nonintersecting spheres—what we might call the kingdom of God and the kingdoms of humankind—in which different rules of conduct apply? Can the Christian be one sort of person in church and another sort of person in government and public life? This cannot be what Jesus meant.

Perhaps Jesus was teaching that the different spheres belong to different types of people. "Pagans" and worldly types, in this understanding, go into the lower world of politics, while the more spiritual types do evangelism, church work, and missions. Given our tendency to drift towards cynicism about politics, Christians might well be tempted to think in such terms. But this cannot be right, for Jesus is the Lord of all.

Jesus commanded us to give Caesar his due, not because he saw Caesar's world as somehow independent from God's, but for the very opposite reason: Jesus knew that his Father reigned as absolute sovereign over every sphere of life, including the political one. God, and God alone, brings men and women and governments (even Rome) into power, and they are to be treated with respect for this very reason. As Paul put it, "Let everyone be subject to the governing authorities, *for* there is no authority except that which God has established" (Romans 13:1, emphasis added).

One Supreme Authority: The Bible's Consistent Message

Neither Jesus nor Paul initiated this notion. Even during the days of the theocracy, God repeatedly taught and demonstrated his universal reign:

> "Look at the nations and watch—and be utterly amazed. For I am going to do something in your days that you would not believe, even if you were told. I am raising up the Babylonians, that ruthless and impetuous people, who sweep across the whole earth to seize dwelling places not their own" (Habakkuk 1:5–6).

The nation to which Habakkuk refers here was the sixth century BC equivalent of Nazi Germany. He describes them as "ruthless," as a "law to themselves," with "horses swifter than leopards" (remember the blitzkrieg?), as "guilty people, whose own strength is their god" (Habakkuk 1:6–8, 11). What shocks and troubles the prophet most deeply is neither the impending judgment on Israel, nor the ruthless evil of the Babylonians. His grief arises from God's assertion that he is going to raise up this people, for Habakkuk rightly contends, "My God, my Holy One....your eyes are too pure to look on evil; you cannot tolerate wrongdoing" (Habakkuk 1:12–13). While admitting the mystery here and acknowledging that God is not to be blamed for the evil that people do to each other, we must also agree that no nation—not even an evil one—arises apart from God's holy and wise administration.

Nebuchadnezzar, who reigned in Babylon from 605 to 562 BC, fulfilled the prophecy of Habakkuk. Rising to power after his rout of the Egyptians at Carchemish in 605, he conquered all of Syria and Palestine, including Judah and Jerusalem, which fell to him in 597 after a brutal siege. Of those few who survived the carnage and famine, nearly all were transported to Babylon.

Then something remarkable happened. For all his arrogant self-assurance, this rapacious monarch came so powerfully under the influence of his godly captives and their Lord that he learned to praise him. The Lord made him mad for a season, and, upon his return to sanity, he wrote:

> I praised the Most High; I honored and glorified him who lives forever. His dominion is an eternal dominion; his kingdom endures from generation to generation. All the peoples of the earth are regarded as nothing. He does as he pleases with the powers of heaven and the peoples of the earth. (Daniel 4:34–35)

God made clear his reign not only during but also at the end of the exile. Around 750 BC, long before the rise of the Babylonian empire, Isaiah foretold the name of the Persian king who would overthrow the Babylonians in 539 BC and issue a decree permitting Jews to return to Judah:

> This is what the LORD says to his anointed, to Cyrus, whose right hand I take hold of to subdue nations before him and to strip kings of their armor…For the sake of Jacob my servant…I summon you by name and bestow on you a title of honor, though you do not acknowledge me. I am the LORD and there is no other. (Isaiah 45:1, 4–5)

Rulers do not have to know the Lord—or even exist yet—for God to reign over and through them. The great prophet Jeremiah, who lived through much political change and personal misery at the hands of wicked people, summarized well what we have been saying. Pronouncing for the Lord, he said, "With my great power and outstretched arm I made the earth and its people and the animals that are on it, and I give it to anyone I please" (Jeremiah 27:5).

Why the rise of America? Why the collapse of the Soviet Union? Why the rise of Pakistan as a nuclear power? Why did the American Revolution succeed and the French fail? How did the British Isles escape the violent upheaval that the eighteenth century brought to France? Why the triumph of Milosevic's butcheries in Kosovo, and of Gandhi's pacifism in India? How do we explain the political and economic tranquility of Costa Rica when all around her so much of Latin America has endured such chaos? How do we explain the peaceful end to apartheid in South Africa, contrary to all expectation? Why did the twentieth century see the rise of so many genocidal regimes and the twenty-first the rise of suicide bombing as the preferred way to make a political point? The secondary (and not insignificant) reasons are numerous and invite careful analysis, but the deepest cause for all these realities is the Lord himself. For a host of purposes, many of which we cannot understand, God establishes the nations and their rulers. Jesus knew this and taught us for this reason to give them their due.

Eyes to See the Deeper Reality

While we must never submit blindly to any authority (we will discuss civil disobedience later), we should nevertheless give more than grudging support to those whom the Lord has placed over us. Paul counseled slaves this way: "Slaves, obey your earthly masters in everything; and do it, not only when their eye is on you and to curry their favor, but with sincerity of heart and reverence for the Lord. Whatever you do, work at it with all your heart, as working for the Lord, not for human masters....It is the Lord Christ you are serving" (Colossians 3:22–24). (*Note:* Far from a pro-slavery manifesto, these words teach the nature of true freedom. Christian slaves only appear to be serving their earthly masters; they in fact serve Christ and are therefore free from their human master's imperfections and injustices. Paul's words furthermore sow the seeds for emancipation, since the slave's Master is also the slave-owner's Master. The human masters who live under Christ can not help but discover over time that they should not enslave others.)

Paul urged upon slaves the faith to see the Lord's hand behind that of the master, and to draw their hopes for justice and their motivation for service not from the master they could see, but from the one they could not see. Though modern public authority differs dramatically from ancient slave ownership and imperial oversight, the same principle applies to us today. The believer sees God's hand behind the process and respects the authority from the heart, for God's sake.

On one occasion my pastoral duties obliged me to give testimony at a hearing that led to the enforced hospitalization of one of my parishioners.

The hearing took place in a small hospital room adjacent to the place where my friend lay strapped to a gurney for his own protection. In addition to me, the assembly consisted of an elderly, wheelchair-bound judge, a clerk, and two attorneys (one representing the interests of the community and the other of my friend). We chatted in a friendly, if subdued, fashion until the clerk called us to order. At that point a remarkable seriousness, a kind of holiness, settled upon us. I will never forget the sense of accountability that we all (including the judge) seemed to feel as we considered the fate (for a time) of my friend. Though no one mentioned God's name, except in the oath taking, his presence as the "judge behind the judge" was palpable in the deference given to his human counterpart, and in the care and sensitivity with which that counterpart heard the evidence and rendered his decision.

As I drove home afterward, I could not help reflecting on the biblical underpinnings of what I had just experienced. I thanked God for the measure to which those underpinnings still exercise their influence in our country, despite the increasing secularization of our time. Knowing how my friend might have been treated in another time or in a different culture increased my resolve to honor the people who are part of the governing process in America.

Beyond the Merely Legal

In early 2009 the news broke that the executives of A.I.G., a massive insurance company, were to receive multimillion-dollar bonuses. This infuriated the public because, first of all, the company was heavily implicated in the mortgage scandal that helped cause the economy to plummet. Secondly, the company had been bailed out with billions in taxpayer money only a few months before. Many cried in fury, "How can we possibly see ourselves paying vast bonuses, from our pockets, to crooks largely responsible for our present woes? It is outrageous!" What stirred up the heat was the discovery that the bonuses were written into contracts that had been drawn up before the earlier bailout, and there appeared to be no legal way to force the executives to give the bonuses back. No doubt spurred on by their constituencies, members of Congress proposed taxing the bonuses at a rate of ninety percent.

And then something wonderful happened. Most of the executives voluntarily returned their bonuses. What motivated this choice most deeply we do not know. But notice what happened. The right thing triumphed over the merely legal thing. The executives were not legally bound to return the money, but they did it anyway. And it was very good for the country.

Why should I pay taxes? Why should I treat with respect the officer who has just given me a $75 speeding ticket? Why do I treat with respect the officer who has just rudely cited me for something I did not do (I will never forget this happening to me as a teenager)? Why do I obey the law? Why, like Esther, Daniel, Paul, and (to cite a modern example) Dietrich Bonhoeffer, do I speak with respect to my captors?[27] Why does my church office obey copyright laws in its production of the worship bulletin and teaching materials? Why do I fight willingly in the armed forces when called unless for reasons of conscience I feel I cannot? And why, if I am a conscientious objector, am I humbly prepared to take the legal consequences for my stand?

Do I act in these ways simply because I might get into trouble if I do not? In other words, is my civic behavior limited only by the question, "Can I get away with it?" Should we respect government and its agents only when we agree with them? Should we honor them only because they do not at the moment interfere with our private rights and pleasures? Not if we are faithful to Scripture. We respect "Caesar" because we respect God; when we dishonor "Caesar" we dishonor God.

Too many Americans, including Christian Americans, seem content these days with satisfying the letter of the civil law. The phenomenal rise in litigation owes itself in large part to our willingness to be content with asking nothing more than "Is it legal?" and "Is it acceptable?" We should also ask "Is it moral?" and "Is it good for the community in which God has placed me?" Because we live under Christ, we should have a conscience attuned to whether a course of action is right before God, not simply tolerable before people. And our conscience should apply itself across the board, in every part of life: environmental concerns, family and marriage issues, energy, medical ethics, business practices, social welfare, awards in liability cases, and so on.

Is it right, I must ask, to sue my town for $10 million simply because I know I can win? Should a Christian builder feel free to build in an environmentally sensitive place just because it is not against the law? Should Christians search high and low for tax loopholes? Should a Christian CEO order the buyout of a small business without considering the hardship that the people of that company and its customers might experience, simply because it is legal to do so? Is it right for an American-based multinational corporation to avoid paying taxes simply because its legal department finds a lawful way to do so by manipulating loopholes in the tax code? Should a Christian teenager accelerate madly down a neighborhood street full of children, satisfied simply because no speed limit is being broken? Should a Christian play the state lottery simply because it is legal? Should a Christian shop all day on Sunday just because the mall is open for business? Is it okay to watch an X-rated movie or drink myself into oblivion just because I have reached the age at which such behavior is now legal? Should I divorce my spouse just because it is legal to do so? Should a Christian researcher draw stem cells from discarded embryos or experiment on aborted fetal tissue simply because the law permits it? Should a believing couple seek to have a child by in vitro fertilization simply because it is legal, knowing that standard practice leads to many discarded embryos?

I ask these questions gently, knowing that the proper answers are not in every case obvious. Nevertheless, I ask them, as we all should, since what is legal and possible is not necessarily right or best. We must all answer to Christ and not simply to the human magistrate.

No legal system can possibly cover every contingency. This means that when we abandon ourselves to the merely legal we invite not the triumph of the good but the triumph of the skillful, or the equivalent in our day of "might makes right." Knowledge is power in our technology-dominated culture. Most things and events (even people) are seen as complex machines requiring experts to unlock their secrets. One such machine is modern legal practice. The legal practitioner who can work the system the best comes out on top.

Furthermore, abandoning ourselves to the merely legal threatens the community, both in the act itself and in its results. A community whose members ask only "Is it legal?" is like a family whose members ask only "Can I get away with this?" It is like a church whose members take each other to court (see 1 Corinthians 6). None will last long. A community of any sort whose members ask only "Is it legal?" discovers that the only way to solve disputes is by suing, a process that may give some satisfaction but rarely improves relationships. How, we must ask, can a community of adversaries be a community?

Godliness Is the Key to Civic Health

Such tragic fallout should be cause enough for us never to be content with the merely legal. But there is a deeper reason still. We serve Christ, and for that reason we care always and most deeply about what is right. I know that the law cannot make me love my neighbor as myself, but I do so anyway because America's laws do not alone bind me.

The eighteenth-century French philosopher Jean-Jacques Rousseau wrote, "Far from winning the hearts of the citizens for the state, [the Christian faith] removes them from it, as from all earthly things. I know nothing that is more actively opposed to the social spirit."[28] We have been noting something quite different. Despite Rousseau's concern over divided loyalties, the Christian turns out in fact to be an excellent citizen. Daniel Webster said, "Whatever makes men good Christians makes them good citizens." Reformation leader John Calvin wrote, "The obedience to leaders and magistrates is always linked to the worship and fear of God." We love our country, not because we worship it (no faithful Christian could do that), nor because it is always right (no wise Christian would ever admit that), but because we trust the divine wisdom of the sovereign one who has placed us where we are and commanded us to love our neighbor in that place. To use the apostle Paul's words, "it is necessary to submit to the authorities, not only because of possible punishment but also as a matter of conscience" (Romans 13:5). Charles Colson summarizes well what we have been saying:

> Christians who are faithful to Scripture should be patriots in the best sense of that word. They are "the salvation of the common-wealth," said Augustine, for they fulfill the highest role of citizenship. Not because they are forced to or even choose to, not out of

any chauvinistic motivations or allegiances to a political leader, but because they love and obey the King who is above all temporal leaders...Since the state cannot legislate love, Christian citizens bring a humanizing element to civic life, helping to produce the spirit by which people do good out of compassion, not compulsion.[29]

An extraordinary revival, later called The Great Awakening, swept through the American colonies in the 1740s. What distinguishes that revival from its often frothy and superficial counterpart in our day was its civic impact. Historian Benjamin Tremble wrote:

> There seemed to be a general conviction, that all the ways of man were before the eyes of the Lord. It was the opinion of men of discernment and sound judgment, who had the best opportunities of knowing the feelings and general state of the people for that period, that bags of gold and silver...might, with safety, have been laid in the streets, and that no man would have converted them to his own use. Theft, wantonness, intemperance, profaneness, Sabbath-breaking, and other gross sins, seemed to be put away.[30]

Imagine what sort of a nation we might be today if in significant numbers we were to bring our public behavior under the scrutiny of a biblically educated conscience. Imagine, in other words, what it might be like if God were deeply feared by many Americans, not in response to a top-down government mandate (that would be impossible), but in response to heart-changing divine impact. Though utopia would still elude us, things would improve, perhaps dramatically. As more people at every level of cultural influence began policing themselves and the communities in which they are involved, crime would diminish, along with the cost of law enforcement and incarceration. Bad debts would diminish as more people found trusting contentment in what they have and chose for that reason not to live beyond their means. Better stories would find their way to TV and screen as screenwriters and producers worked harder to find and tell them. Greater openness to the things that please God would find its way to the editorial pages of leading newspapers. Universities would welcome an intelligent theism into the marketplace of ideas. The pornography industry would shrivel up, as would human trafficking, because demand would drop off dramatically. Domestic violence, both physical and psychological, would begin to give way before the happy pressure of love and faithfulness, with incalculable benefits to children (and to their children after them). The demand for drugs would diminish as increasing numbers of people found meaning and love under the reign of Christ. Streets, sky, and rivers would be cleaner as more people thought twice about polluting God's earth. Integrity in business would be more common, reducing the necessity for bureaucratic monitoring and litigation, both of which absorb colossal amounts of time, energy, and money. Hope and trust would exercise a stronger influence upon the tone of public discourse, occasioning more courtesy and less accusation, more creativity and less complaint, more optimism and less cynicism. Mercy, generosity, goodness, and justice, rising freely from every corner of the culture—from "regular" people and the elite alike—would build the sort of quality community that government could never successfully impose.

We are to give "Caesar" his due. What is that? What do we "owe" America? Certainly not worship. Certainly not blind allegiance. What we owe America is our love, for the Lord we worship gave our country its life and placed us in her midst, filling her with people whom he commands us to love as we love ourselves. We must begin by loving one another in the church—but we must push beyond the church into all our relationships. America isn't an institution (or series of institutions) to be tolerated or somehow gotten around. It is people seeking to find a way to live together—people we must learn to love for Christ's sake. We would be foolish to expect that our love will produce heaven on earth; we must await Christ's return for that. But we would be equally wrong to deny the power of Christ to work significant change upon our land should we commit ourselves to push past the selfishness that is natural to us.

Making It Personal

1. Winston Churchill made the following observation before the House of Commons on November 11, 1947: "It has been said that democracy is the worst form of government—except for all those other forms that have been tried from time to time." Discuss Churchill's remark in the light of Romans 13:1–7, a text that describes government as a "necessary evil" instituted by God to keep human beings from social self-destruction. Why, according to Romans 13, is human government necessary? What "evils" do human governments contribute to? Think not only of foreign governments but also of the United States: campaign financing, prison population demographics, taxation policies, racial profiling.

2. View the film *Dead Man Walking* and discuss capital punishment in the light of the film and the following passages: Genesis 9:5–6, Matthew 5:38–45, and Romans 13:1-7. Some questions to consider: (a) Could the nun have been as effective in reaching the murderer if she had believed that capital punishment was morally justifiable? (b) Would the murderer have come to admit his crime if he did not know that he was going to die? (c) Does the film depict capital punishment as a "necessary evil"? (d) Does Scripture call the parents of the slain teenagers to respond to the murderer in the same way that it calls the government to respond to him? (e) What particulars about America's practice of capital punishment need reform?

3. Look back to the section of this chapter entitled "Beyond the Merely Legal" where you will find a list of ethical questions, beginning with, "Is it right to ask…." Try to develop a thoughtful answer to at least one of those questions. As you do so, try to articulate (a) what circumstances might modify your answer, (b) what effect different attitudes of heart might have on your answer, (c) what further facts you would need to know before you could answer, and (d) what biblical principles and passages might apply to the issue.

4. Reread the statement by Charles Colson in the section titled "Godliness Is the Key to Civic Health". Share some examples of things you have each done freely for the public good—not because the laws of America required it, and not because you were afraid of getting in trouble if you did not do it, but simply because you knew it was pleasing to God and helpful to your community.

"Love the Lord your God with all your heart and with all your soul and with all your mind." This is the first and greatest commandment. (Matthew 22:37–38)

Do not suppose that I have come to bring peace to the earth. I did not come to bring peace, but a sword. For I have come to turn "a man against his father, a daughter against her mother, a daughter-in-law against her mother-in-law—a man's enemies will be the members of his own household." Anyone who loves their father or mother more than me is not worthy of me; anyone who loves their son or daughter more than me is not worthy of me. Whoever does not take up their cross and follow me is not worthy of me. Whoever finds their life will lose it, and whoever loses their life for my sake will find it. (Matthew 10:34–39)

He who surrenders himself without reservation to the temporal claims of a nation, or a party, or a class is rendering to Caesar that which, of all things, most emphatically belongs to God: himself. ("Learning in War-Time," C. S. Lewis)

Chapter 7

GIVING GOD HIS DUE

Near the beginning of *The Sum of All Fears*, Tom Clancy introduces us to Father Tim Riley, a savvy Jesuit who teaches at Georgetown. When asked about Father Tim's trustworthiness regarding a delicate matter of state, CIA deputy director Jack Ryan answers, "Father Tim is an American citizen, and he's not a security risk. But he's also a priest, and he has taken vows to what he naturally considers an authority higher than the Constitution. You can trust the man to honor all his obligations, but don't forget what all those obligations are."[31]

We must not forget what all our obligations are. We must love America for Christ's sake, not for her own sake, which means that we will love her deeply but neither blindly nor absolutely. Our deepest obligation will always be to Christ. Christ spoke of bringing a sword, not because his prime intention was to divide people from each other, but because he knew that the allegiance he demanded would inevitably lead to that division.

Consider again the dispute over paying taxes to Caesar. If the Roman denarius belonged to Caesar because it bore the impress of his image, to whom do you suppose we belong, given the image we bear by creation and, if Christian, by redemption? (See Genesis 1:26; Romans 8:29.) Though Jesus did not make this point explicitly in that interchange, we can be sure from his treatment of people and his loyalty to Scripture that he believed it.[32] We belong absolutely to the King of all kings and our efforts to be good citizens express that deeper loyalty. For this reason, we respectfully refuse to obey "Caesar" when he commands of us something that Scripture forbids. (We will discuss this more fully in chapter nine.)

I had to grapple with this issue during my last year in college. The Vietnam War had escalated to the point that there were no longer draft deferments for those who, like me, were contemplating graduate school. What is worse, a national draft lottery had given me a low number, which all but guaranteed that I would be drafted upon graduation. What was I as a follower of Jesus to do? Certainly I did not want to risk losing my life, especially since I was engaged to be married. But I knew that this fear did not constitute a legitimate reason for denying my country its due. In addition, I was genuinely confused about the ethics of the conflict. I believed in just war theory (we discussed this in chapter five), but found myself wondering about the fundamental justice of our involvement in Vietnam. As it turned out, while still struggling with the ethics of it all, I flunked my army physical and received a permanent exemption. But for this eleventh hour development I may well have had respectfully to refuse to serve my country out of love for Jesus.

Promoting What Pleases God

Refusing "Caesar" when we are morally and spiritually compelled to is only half our responsibility. If I am to "give to God what is God's," especially in our democratic country, I will work to bring his standards to bear upon it. That is, I will love America enough to promote those things that please our heavenly King and resist those things that displease him. I will be an active citizen, never assuming that something is right simply because I am comfortable with it, or because it is American. In this sense, Rousseau's concern about the "divided loyalty" of Christian citizens noted in chapter six has a certain basis: "Jesus came in order to set up a spiritual kingdom on earth; thereby the theological system was separated from the political system, and this in turn meant that the state ceased to be *one* state, and that inherent tension emerged, which has never since ceased to agitate the Christian peoples."[33]

Legislating Morality

Working for social change can take many forms, as we shall see in subsequent chapters. Let us consider for the moment one possible way: legislation.

May a Christian seek to advance a wealth tax on the top 1% because his faith convinces him that such a tax is just? May a Christian promote policies that make it unfeasible for women's health clinics in her state to offer abortion services because her faith convinces her that the law must protect the unborn? Should a church sponsor a local ordinance that effectively closes down an "adult" book store in its neighborhood? Should a Christian baker seek legal sanction, on the basis of his faith, for refusing to make a wedding cake for a gay couple? Should a Christian seek to shut down a coal mine because he believes that its continuation is in defiance of God's mandate to care for the environment?

There are those who argue that such actions, certainly the religious motivations behind them, threaten the freedom from religious coercion that our Constitution was designed to protect. Christians, they complain, have no right to impose their faith-based morality upon our secular and pluralistic country. Such imposition, they say, breaches the "wall of separation" that properly stands between church and state.

How should Christians respond to such arguments? Is it in fact wrong for them (for us) to seek to legislate morality? By doing so do we fail to love our neighbors as ourselves? The answer is not as simple as some might think. If we concur that we must not do so, we must then ask whether the lordship of Christ really means anything to us. But if we say yes, we must immediately confront other questions, like "Which morals do we seek to legislate and why?" Why, for example, might we promote laws regulating financial behavior and not laws regulating sexual behavior? Why, for that matter, should we legislate against stealing, but not against false worship and hypocrisy—crimes that are particularly heinous to our Lord? And if we promote laws regulating sexual behavior, which sexual behaviors should they target?

Deriving civil laws from Scripture and applying them in modern America demands careful thought beyond the scope of our efforts here. We will have to be content with an observation and three distinctions that should help us navigate the difficult waters.

Everyone Legislates Morality

Those who argue that the law must never promote ethical values are not thinking clearly. After all, what are the laws of our nation if they are not the legal expression of the values that we hold? By prohibiting theft, drunk driving, Ponzi schemes, and child abuse, and by writing standards for commerce, affirmative action, environmental protection, and divorce proceedings, people codify the values that they believe in. Those who cry "You must not legislate morality" are themselves advocating a certain set of values (a moral position is implicit in the word "must") and bringing it to bear upon the process of lawmaking.

We simply cannot escape the influence of values. They may be good values or bad values, depending upon our perspective, but they will always be the basis upon which we do our lawmaking. When, therefore, people cry "How dare you legislate morality?" what they really mean is "How dare you legislate *that* particular morality, since I disagree with it?" The useful question is not *whether* ethics should be enforced by law, since that goes on all the time, but rather *which* ethics should be. And Christian people, like anybody else, have a right and responsibility to stand up legislatively for the values that please their heavenly King. After all, if they do not, who will? Edmund Burke said, "The only thing necessary for the triumph of evil is for good men to do nothing."

Distinguishing between Theocracy and Influence

Questions of course still remain for the Christian. He still must decide which of God's values should be enforced by law and which by other means. He must sort out which legislation advances God's values in the best way. And he must reckon with the likely fact that Christian brothers and sisters will disagree with his legislative agenda. Navigating these waters can be difficult. How do we do it?

First, we must lean against the tendency to try to make America Christian by force of law. We must distinguish in other words between the Christian takeover of government (the theocratic impulse) and the Christian influence upon government.

Some of us are nostalgic about what we perceive to have been a "Christian golden age" and this dream fires us with zeal to recapture that past. While it is true that Christianity enjoyed for many years a privileged position in public life (often to the benefit of that life), those times were not without their problems. The community that had fled England in search of religious freedom drove Roger Williams from its borders because he championed freedom of conscience and justice for those who were here before the Europeans arrived. Thomas Jefferson (one of many Deists among the Founding Fathers) excised large portions of his Bible to conform it to his less-than-orthodox faith. And slavery was both tolerated and defended until after the mid-nineteenth century.

The present even more than the past should check our zeal to force Christianity upon our land. The American population today is far more diverse both ethnically and religiously than it once was. The concern in the eighteenth century was that no particular brand of Christianity should gain political ascendancy; today America welcomes a seemingly endless variety of faiths—religious and nonreligious. Any approach taken by Christians to promote the values of Christ in public life must deal with this reality. If we seek to circumvent pluralism in the name of Christ, or to blast a path through it, we will in the end produce a culture that tolerates a Christian presence even less than it does now.

The most important reason not to make America legally Christian is that God forbids us to. We noted earlier that theocracy belongs to an earlier stage in redemptive history, when God's kingdom was identified with a particular earthly kingdom. Edmund Clowney writes:

> No state, no freedom fighter today can lay claim to Israel's theocratic calling as warriors of God's covenant. The new Israel is the church of Jesus Christ, and he has forbidden the sword to the church. Under the lordship of Christ the Kingdom of God does take form in the church, but through mightier weapons than the sword: weapons,

as Paul affirms, that can reduce every towering imagination of the rebellious human heart. No other weapons can advance Christ's Kingdom. The political renovation of the world awaits his return, for he is the sole monarch of the universe.[34]

Jesus wields a sword today, but it comes from his mouth and not his arm (see Revelation 1:16), a vivid reminder that the sort of allegiance he seeks cannot be forced. It must be chosen freely out of love in response to his word. This does not mean that Christians may never seek to legislate morality. But it does mean that when we do, we need to understand the limits of what we are doing. We are not building the kingdom of God. We are giving our best shot at trying to make the world a little bit better.

We must struggle to distinguish in thought and practice between trying to make America God's nation by force of law (which is mistaken) and seeking to use lawful means in a sensitive way to promote values that please Christ (which is a good thing—though limited in its effect). A pithy summary of Christian influence upon American culture appeared in PBS President Ervin Duggan's remarks at the Davidson College 1994 fall convocation:

> Only years after leaving this place did I realize that the religious tradition honored by those starchy old Calvinists [Davidson's founders] was what brought into being many of the things I cherished most. The teaching that all persons are created in the image of God, for example: that religious idea gives the only transcendent depth and meaning to our notions of human rights, of human beings as sacred. The ancient doctrine of Original Sin, for example: it led James Madison and John Adams to insist upon limitations of power, upon a system of checks and balances. The Judeo-Christian idea of covenantal laws and relationships, for example: this led, in time, to modern democratic constitutions and the Bill of Rights. Indeed, our modern ideas of tolerance and pluralism owe much to great assertions of human universality like that of St. Paul: "I am persuaded that in Christ, there is neither Jew nor Greek."[35]

Though we may find the distinction between theocracy and influence difficult to make in the nitty-gritty, and though we may find ourselves disagreeing with each other in the effort, we nevertheless must humbly try.

Distinguishing between Private and Corporate Callings

I remember leaving my church in Virginia early one Sunday afternoon and discovering that during the service a well-intentioned church member had placed leaflets promoting a particular pro-life candidate on every windshield in the parking lot. When asked by the church leadership not to do this sort of thing again, the member was genuinely mystified. Her mystification grew in part from her failure to distinguish sufficiently between the responsibility of the individual Christian citizen and the responsibility of the institutional church.

A member of my New York church was as troubled over the war with Iraq as was the parking lot lobbyist over the killing of the unborn. It was unfathomable to him that any Christian would speak out against abortion while remaining supportive of (or even silent about) a war that was, in his view, built upon a flimsy rationale, driven largely by greed, and responsible for the death of tens of thousands of civilians. Had he confused private and corporate callings as the parking lot lobbyist did, he would have leafleted the church with anti-war flyers.

Chapter three describes the primary calling of the church, a calling from which political matters must not divert her; but individual Christians, working alone and in conjunction with others, have more diverse callings. I must discern and pursue my particular calling, faithful to the one who intends to rule my whole life, both private and public. At the same time, I must not expect my church to adopt my calling and follow along after me, as if my priorities and those of my church ought to be precisely the same. The parking lot lobbyist had wrongly assumed that her calling, her sense of priority, and her convictions on how best to advance that priority could be legitimately imposed upon the church family as a whole.

Distinguishing between Principles and Strategies

This brings us to a third distinction that helps navigate the shoals of legislating morality—the distinction between principles and strategies. Shortly after Ronald Reagan's election, one of the deacons in my church rose up in public worship and publicly thanked God with these words: "O Lord, we bless you that at last your man is in the White House." His prayer drew a fiery response from a church member that mystified him. His surprise grew from the failure sufficiently to draw this third distinction. The institutional church (and the individual believer as well) must speak out on the standards and values that the King of the church loves. But the moment we move into the realm of strategy—the moment we begin to wrestle with just how we are to bring those standards and values to bear upon our culture—we must be careful, humble, and gracious with one another.

My deacon was entitled to his conviction that Ronald Reagan was the best man for the White House at the time (just as someone might believe that Barack Obama was the best man for 2008 or Donald Trump for 2016). But he needed to hold that conviction loosely and take care as a leader in the church not to place divine sanction upon a fallen and imperfect instrument. God's law (the source of our highest principles) must not be compromised, but its application in public life (what we are calling strategies) must be left to the individual operating freely under the reign of Christ. One of the Scriptures' high principles is the sanctity of the human conscience in areas where biblical prescriptions are unclear or incomplete—and politics is invariably such an area. (See Romans 14 and 1 Corinthians 8 for discussions on the conscience.)

During the Nazi era, the church as the church had an obligation to resist Hitler in areas where he plainly broke God's law. The Confessing Church influenced by Bonhoeffer did just that, witnessed by the courageous resistance of the 1934 Barman Declaration, part of which follows:

1. Jesus Christ, as he is attested for us in Holy Scripture, is the one Word of God which we have to hear and which we have to trust and obey in life and in death. We reject the false teaching that the church could and would acknowledge any other events and powers, figures

and truths, as God's revelation, or as a source of its proclamation, apart from and besides this one Word of God…

3. The Christian church is the congregation of brothers and sisters in which Jesus Christ acts presently as the Lord in Word and sacrament, through the Holy Spirit. As the church of forgiven sinners, it has to bear witness in the midst of a sinful world, with both its faith and its obedience, with its proclamation as well as its order, that it is the possession of him alone, and that it lives and wills to live only from his comfort and his guidance in the expectation of his appearance. We reject the false teaching, that the church is free to abandon the form of its proclamation and order in favor of anything it pleases, or in response to prevailing ideological or political beliefs.[36]

It was right (if dangerous) for the church to assert its independence from the state in this way. But Bonhoeffer's disturbing decision to participate in the attempt on Hitler's life was a "strategy" that he, rightly, never asked the church to adopt.

Two Hot-Button Issues

Two hot topics for Christians are abortion and (increasingly) climate change. The church must urge us to love our neighbors as ourselves. Those neighbors will include the unborn children whose lives are at risk because of Roe v. Wade (together with any women whose lives are at risk because of difficult or unwanted pregnancies);[37] they will also include the children of future generations, together with the world's poor, who will be adversely affected by the rising sea levels and the severe weather patterns brought on by the heating of the planet.[38] But the church must also urge us to make room for a host of different legitimate strategies (legislative and otherwise) for advancing our love for neighbor in both areas.

Consider climate change. Christians may genuinely disagree on the best way to address it. Some may vigorously seek to advance the Green New Deal, lobbying friends and legislators to embrace it. Others may choose a slower, more pragmatic approach, advancing only those initiatives that are likely to gain broad enough support to move things forward. Still others may choose to throw their energy into helping local churches set an example by "greening" their facilities and urging their people to reduce their carbon footprints dramatically.

With regard to abortion there are numerous strategies for ending or reducing it. Some choose to take direct action: they vote for pro-life candidates, or they picket abortion clinics, or they offer sidewalk counseling to women as they approach a clinic, or they support state laws that severely restrict abortions in hopes that the likely appeals against those laws will eventuate in a Supreme Court hearing. [39] There are, on the other hand, some Christians who are not persuaded that direct action is the most effective route. They argue that abortions have tended, ironically, to rise during pro-life administrations because the social policies during those administrations have tended to make it harder for women with troubled pregnancies to carry their children to term. They choose action that makes things easier on the mothers—action that can include supporting crisis pregnancy centers, adoption services, and even voting for pro-choice candidates—not necessarily because the candidates are pro-choice but because they support social policies that reduce the need for abortions. Still other believers choose to focus their efforts on dialogue with the opposition in hopes of finding a common ground that will at least reduce abortions.

Vive La Difference

Strategies vary tremendously, and believers should learn how to discuss those differences with each other in a spirit of love and humility. We should also bear with those church leaders who are reticent to endorse, or even to appear to endorse, one particular strategy, understanding that such endorsement fails to account for the diversity of gifts and callings which God gives his people and can divide the church where it should not be divided.

A good exercise, though it must be entered into thoughtfully and with much prayer, is to hold church-wide public discussions on hot social issues, the purpose being twofold: to help one another distinguish between principles and strategies, and to learn how to debate and to disagree peaceably. The latter purpose is as important as the former, since we have been called to model the kingdom of God by our love. If we (in whom Christ dwells) cannot lovingly disagree, how can we expect the culture around us to?

A church I once served had a large medical population in its membership—medical students, medical school faculty and administrators, nurses, practicing physicians, and public health officials. Knowing that contemporary issues in medical ethics were on everyone's mind, we determined to have a class on the subject. We also knew that many of the issues involved were hot ones, potentially destructive to the fellowship of our church, so we proceeded cautiously. To prepare for it, a dozen of us (including myself as the resident "theologian," the head of public health in the region, an administrator, some nurses, a researcher, and a number of practicing physicians) spent nearly a year together, studying and hammering out an understanding on a broad range of issues. The resulting class proved to be of immense help to scores of believers who were struggling with tough issues but were afraid to air them in church for fear of controversy.

Another church I served routinely held Sunday evening panel discussions on hot topics. The wide range of issues included racism in the church, war, homosexuality, and women's leadership in the church and society. We generally chose the panelists from among ourselves so as to avoid a professional debate between outsiders. The aim was to learn how to speak honestly and charitably among ourselves.

William Wilberforce: A Model for Us

William Wilberforce grew up at a time when slavery flourished in the British Empire. Appalled by the practice, the young believer determined to fight it. Since he was a member of parliament and a gifted orator (providential realities that helped determine his public calling), Wilberforce settled upon a legislative strategy—to go after the institution indirectly by first going after the slave trade. Humbled by his own complicity in the sin and by a keen sense

of inadequacy, he opened the struggle in 1787 with a speech in the House
of Commons:

> When I consider the magnitude of the subject which I am to bring
> before the House—a subject, in which the interest, not of this coun-
> try, nor of Europe alone, but of the whole world, and of posterity,
> are involved...it is impossible for me not to feel both terrified and
> concerned at my own inadequacy to such a task...But I march
> forward with a firmer step in the full assurance that my cause will
> bear me out....I mean not to accuse anyone, but to take the shame
> upon myself, in common, indeed, with the whole Parliament of
> Great Britain, for having suffered this horrid trade to be carried on
> under their authority. We are all guilty—we ought all to plead guilty,
> and not to exculpate ourselves by throwing the blame on others.[40]

Faced by an economy that depended heavily upon the continuation of
slavery, he nevertheless clung tenaciously to the cause until after twenty years
he saw the slave trade outlawed. For eighteen more years, until his retirement in
1825, Wilberforce fought unsuccessfully for the end of slavery itself. Not until
July 29, 1833, three days before he died, did the bill abolishing slavery pass in
the House of Commons. "Thank God," he whispered before he slipped into a
final coma, "that I should have lived to witness a day in which England was
willing to give twenty millions sterling for the abolition of slavery."[41]

Few of us may ever occupy the place of political influence that Wilberforce
held, and few of us may share his natural abilities. But we can all learn much
from this remarkable statesman, a man whose faith was never disconnected
from his public life. He challenges our pragmatism by being a man of undying
principle who refused to allow staggering opposition and repeated failure to
deter him. He challenges the impatient idealists among us by his patience and
by his savvy willingness to go after slavery by going first after the slave trade
(there is perhaps some wisdom here for the abortion struggle). He challenges
those of us who have forgotten the legitimate role of religion in formulating
public policy by being driven by Christian conviction throughout the struggle.[42]
He challenges those among us who would withdraw from serious controversy,

or simply lob mortars at the opposition, by readily accepting his nation's guilt as his own.

Making It Personal

1. Rousseau articulated a tension Christians often feel: "Jesus came in order to set up a spiritual kingdom on earth; thereby the theological system was separated from the political system, and this in turn meant that the state ceased to be *one* state, and that inherent tension emerged, which has never since ceased to agitate the Christian peoples." Discuss examples from your experience in which you have felt torn between allegiance to God and allegiance to your country. How did you resolve the tension?

2. In the fall of 1999 New York Mayor Rudolph Giuliani sought to withhold city funds from the Brooklyn Museum when the museum chose to exhibit a painting of the Virgin Mary covered with cow dung. Some saw his action as a triumph for decency and godly values. Others saw it as an infringement on the freedom of expression. Still others complained that the mayor's action was foolish, playing into the publicity scheme of the exhibit's promoters. Was the mayor right to impose his views (and those of others) on the Brooklyn Museum?

3. Read the following excerpt from the chapter: "We simply cannot escape the influence of values. They may be good values or bad values, depending upon our perspective, but they will always be the basis upon which we do our lawmaking. When, therefore, people cry 'How dare you legislate morality?' what they really mean is 'How dare you legislate *that* particular morality, since I disagree with it?' The useful question

is not *whether* ethics should be enforced by law, since that goes on all the time, but rather *which* ethics should be."

Discuss which sorts of social values should be enforced by law and which should be promoted by other means. Try to develop a rationale for the distinction.

4. According to this chapter, three distinctions will help us think though the complex issue of legislating morality: (a) the distinction between Christian influence and Christian theocracy, (b) the distinction between the calling of the church as a whole and the calling of the individual Christian, and (c) the distinction between moral principle and political strategy. Discuss what is meant by these three distinctions. Try to develop a plan for addressing a hot social issue that takes all of these distinctions into consideration.

5. Read over the final paragraph of the chapter, where the challenge of William Wilberforce is summarized. Evaluate your own social and political involvements in the light of Wilberforce's example. Which are you more like: the pragmatist (who tends to give up because the odds are long), the impatient idealist (who demands perfection immediately), the secularist (one who "has forgotten the legitimate role of religion in…public policy"), or the "withdrawer" (who "simply lobs mortars at the opposition" and refuses to accept "his nation's guilt as his own")?

My soul glorifies the Lord and my spirit rejoices in God my Savior, for he has been mindful of the humble state of his servant. From now on all generations will call me blessed, for the Mighty One has done great things for me—holy is his name. His mercy extends to those who fear him, from generation to generation. He has performed mighty deeds with his arm; he has scattered those who are proud in their inmost thoughts. He has brought down rulers from their thrones but has lifted up the humble. He has filled the hungry with good things but has sent the rich away empty. He has helped his servant Israel, remembering to be merciful to Abraham and his descendants forever, just as he promised our ancestors. (Luke 1:46–55)

Chapter 8

MAKING A DIFFERENCE: THREE APPROACHES

I had never thought much about abortion until I heard C. Everett Koop, later to become the United States Surgeon General, address the issue in the late seventies. His lecture convinced my wife and me that our country was implicated in an enormous social evil and we had to do something about it. But what? We hardly knew where to begin. It dawned on my wife after some reflection that she needed to part company with her gynecologist. This was not easy, since she was pregnant with our first child, and he was a fine and attentive physician. But he actively promoted abortion rights, and she could not in good conscience continue with him. Together we wrote him, communicating both our appreciation of his care and the reason for our departure from that care. He responded, as we expected he would (this is what made leaving him difficult), with a kind and gracious letter, explaining his position and wishing us well.

A number of years later, during the flap over the fatal decision a three-year-old's parents made to replace his conventional chemotherapy with something experimental, I wrote the following letter to the editor of *The Boston Globe*:

> What is so striking is all the medical and legal uproar over the life
> of one child when seen in the context of the legally and medically
> sanctioned destruction of tens of thousands of unborn children in

101

Boston area hospitals and clinics since 1973. Imagine for a moment that a test had predicted Chad's condition before he was born. Current wisdom might well have urged his destruction "in utero" to save the family years of heartache and expense. Since he was three years out of the womb, however, everything is different. Now the parents are at best incompetent and at worst wicked. If Chad's parents had shown "consistently bad judgment, which endangered the life of their child" (Judge Hennessey), what of the rest of us who have deliberately destroyed, or silently permitted the destruction of, so many unborn children? If we are truly concerned about preserving life, then let's do so consistently. [43]

In the mid-eighties, as the abortion debate continued to swell, I grew increasingly troubled by the pro-choice complaint, often justified, that the pro-lifers showed little concern for the mothers. One Sunday I preached on the subject and was delighted when, following the service, four University of Virginia law students approached me asking what they could do. I really had no idea but agreed to meet with them and talk over lunch. To my amazement they ended up spearheading a "pro-mother" initiative that led to the establishment of the Charlottesville Crisis Pregnancy Center, a sensitive, practical, and professional ministry to women with troubling pregnancies.

Most personally rewarding of all of our involvements in the pro-life cause was our relationship with Anne. A college undergraduate, pregnant out of wedlock by a man who had no long-term interest in her, Anne was under enormous pressure from family and friends to have an abortion when she came to us. She elected to keep the baby and we elected to take her in. A woman in our church offered to be her Lamaze partner, accompanying her to all the classes and attending at the birth. Anne went on to finish her undergraduate studies, marry, and have at least one other child. A picture of her and her first child for many years adorned our refrigerator door.

Many Avenues

This brief account of my wife's and my involvement in a particular cause underscores something of the variety of avenues open to us as we work for change. Few of us have either the gifts or the opportunities that William Wilberforce had. But this should not discourage us, for legislative action at a national level is only one of many ways to bring change. We serve a great God who works his will at every conceivable level of life and who especially likes to humble our proud hearts by working the greatest changes through the most unlikely means.

Think about Mary the mother of Jesus, whose famous song appears at the head of this chapter. A young Jewish woman in an occupied and male-dominated society, she had no social influence at all. Yet God called her to bear the one who would one day change everything. Filled with wonder she sang of a God who scatters the proud, puts down the mighty, and sends the "rich away empty," while caring for and even exalting those who, like her, have no social clout.

Like Gideon's tiny band we are a strange army. But under God's hand we can influence America profoundly. Consider some of the ways we can make a difference. We can pray for change. We can talk up change, seeking to persuade by reasoned argument. Or we can live out change, seeking to demonstrate its wisdom by example. We can protest what we deem an unjust law, or seek to change it by legislative process. We can create the appetite for change through the arts (Billie Holiday's *Strange Fruit*, a haunting jazz number about lynching, stirred our national conscience). Or we can go after social change indirectly but most radically by throwing ourselves into evangelism. And we can work for change at a variety of different social levels, beginning with the smallest community (alone on our knees) and ranging upward from a conversation over coffee to a national debate. We must not mistakenly assume that the only road open to us is the limited-access highway of power politics (a way that, despite appearances, affects the deep things of culture only slightly). In a day when so many complain about their lack of empowerment, the believer who faithfully does what he or she can do, at whatever level, need neither worry nor complain.

Charles D. Drew

The First Approach: Respect People

As we work, a number of important approaches should help—some of them attitudes, some of them strategies. We will consider five, three in this chapter and two in the next. They are respect, cooperation, diversity, integrity, and simplicity.

First, there is respect. We must, in other words, keep public life human. Whatever we do as American citizens we must always act upon our King's operating principle that people are more important than politics or power. God used Mary for his purposes, but he never used her as a cog in his cosmic machine. He spoke kindly to her through Gabriel, commending her and explaining what he was about to do. He sent the prophet Simeon to foretell her anguish. As Jesus hung dying, he saw to her comfort and protection by appointing John to look after her. In the Lord's *modus operandi*, the cosmic and the intimate, the big picture and the tiniest vignette of human experience, come together. People have always mattered and will always matter supremely to him, even as he works out his great purposes.

Jesus' and the Apostles' Examples

First Peter 2:13 literally reads, "Submit yourselves for the Lord's sake to every human creature." Commenting on this statement, Edmund Clowney points out that "Peter is not talking about submission to institutions, but submission to people."[44] Peter humanizes public life in keeping with God's priority. In doing so he articulates what Christ demonstrated. For Jesus political figures were not merely (or even primarily) functionaries to be used, tolerated, placated, or somehow gotten around. They were individuals, people made in God's image, who needed to know the heavenly King.

You perhaps remember the story of Nicodemus in John 3. Nicodemus was a Pharisee and a member of the Jewish ruling council, a member in other words of that group of people who were Jesus' religious and political enemies. Jesus criticized this group with such skill and vehemence that they came to hate him passionately and eventually killed him. Yet, when Nicodemus came to Jesus by night, the Lord received him with respect and directness. Jesus treated him not as a member of a particular group, but as a person in his own right.

Paul followed his master's example when he was examined before King Agrippa. On trial for his life, he appeared in chains. Despite the adversarial setting, Paul brought the interview to an end with sincere and simple words: "I pray to God that not only you but all who are listening to me today may become what I am, except for these chains" (Acts 26:29). For Paul, Agrippa was above all a person for whom the prisoner wanted the very best.

Politics Is People—One at a Time

Such an attitude differs dramatically from what has characterized much of the social and political dealings in our times. M. Y. Latsis, a leader in Lenin's secret police, chillingly wrote:

> We are not carrying out war against individuals. We are extermi-
> nating the bourgeoisie as a class. We are not looking for evidence
> or witnesses to reveal deeds or words against the Soviet power. The
> first question we ask is—to what class does he belong, what are his
> origins, upbringing, education, and profession? These questions
> define the fate of the accused.[45]

Lenin's decree of 1918 called on agencies of the state to "purge the Russian land of all kinds of harmful insects," and included in the list, according to Alexsandr Solzhenitsyn, "people in the Cooper movements, homeowners, high-school teachers, parish councils and choirs, priests, monks, and nuns, Tolstoyan pacifists, and officials of trade unions," all soon to be classified as "former people."[46] The Soviet political philosophy led to at least 20 million deaths in Russia and set the precedent for similarly brutal purges in such places as Germany, China, and Cambodia.

With relief and thanksgiving we distance ourselves from such thinking and sometimes forget how easily we gravitate toward less extreme forms of the same thing. McCarthy's anti-Communist movement in the 1950s, the civil rights movement and those who opposed it in the 1960s, the politically correct movement in the 1990s, and the pro-life and pro-choice movements (one could almost pick at random) have all to a greater or lesser extent tended to identify the "enemy" as a group and either repudiated or demonized them. While there is nothing wrong with trying to understand and critique a movement or a government as a whole, we often forget the most important thing—that movements and governments are made up of people.

Though I have never held public office, I was appointed for a number of years to a steering committee whose purpose was to develop goals and standards for education in our school district. Frustrated by the snail's pace at which we often worked and the educational jargon we had to cope with, I often thought of quitting early. God helped me to persist by reminding me that the administrators, teachers, and community leaders with whom I worked were not primarily functionaries. They were creatures made in God's image responsible for the education of children, also made in God's image. They needed the perspective, prayers, and civility that an ambassador of Christ could bring to their work. I find it difficult to measure the success of the steering committee in its appointed task, but I am hopeful that something of the kingdom of God rubbed off on the people I worked with and was a good thing for our community.

Whether we are exercising authority or appealing to it, we do well to take to heart C. S. Lewis's memorable words: "nations, cultures, arts, civilization— these are mortal, and their life is to ours as the life of a gnat." Understanding this about people, we will resist the impulse to draw the human element out of public life. The student I teach, the professor who instructs me, the convicted thief whom I admonish from the bench, the judge who admonishes me, the driver who yells at me because I happen to be sitting behind the window at the DMV, the "bureaucrat" behind the window at the DMV, the constituent who writes me an impassioned letter, the senator whose recent vote infuriates me, the neighbor whose ideas about foreign policy drive me crazy—these are all people made in God's image, "immortal horrors or everlasting splendors."[47]

We must struggle to keep public life human. Endowed with eyes of faith, we look through the bureaucracy and the power structures to the people behind them. We try to look beyond the badge to the heart, and practice respect, not only because of the office represented, but also because of the humanity of the one who wears the badge. We try to look beyond the platform to the people who align themselves with that platform, refusing to pigeonhole or to demean or in any way dehumanize. And when we are in power, we look always to serve: "Live as free people, but do not use your freedom as a cover-up for evil; live as God's slaves. Show proper respect to everyone, love the family of believers, fear God, honor the emperor" (1 Peter 2:16–17). Commenting on these verses, Edmund Clowney says,

> Christ's Lordship...must transform the way Christians exercise authority in [every] sphere of life. Christians will understand that political authority, like church authority, is service under God. Its purpose is the good of those governed, not the glory of the governor or the profit of the governing class. This principle guides Christians who share in governing authority in democracies. Their goal must also be to serve, to seek the good of the whole people, with special concern for the poor and weak [48]

If we must treat public figures with respect, how much more must we do so with one another. The believer who disagrees with you politically is nevertheless your brother in Christ, one for whom Christ died, one with whom you will be spending eternity. Of all people, he must be one whom you refuse to despise. As offensive as you may find his politics, he himself is not the incarnation of them, and you must resist the tendency to reduce him to that.

The Second Approach: Look for Ways to Cooperate

Respect fosters cooperation. If we understand that people always matter the most, we will seek to work *with* people as much as possible. We will struggle to be team players, encouraging others, looking for common ground, giving others the benefit of the doubt, resisting a conspiracy mentality.

We are suspicious people, prone to a "we/they" mindset, a mentality that poisons cooperation in public life. Christ wants us to bring healing, not disease. He calls us to be engaged in drawing the venom from public discourse by the manner in which we exercise our public responsibility.

At first glance Christian theology might seem to speak against cooperation. Scripture tells us that we are at war—that sin, the world, and the devil implacably oppose the interests of God's kingdom. On what basis, then, can Christians work together with a fallen world? Three important ideas answer this question: common grace, total depravity, and human creation in the image of God. The first of these, common grace, maintains that God continues to bless the world with his truth, beauty, and goodness, despite our widespread rejection of him. The second, total depravity, teaches in part that sin shows up everywhere, in everything we do and everyone we meet. Creation in the image of God reminds us, as we have already noted, that every person matters profoundly.

A conspiracy mentality denies all three of these ideas, for multiple reasons. In the first place it closes the mind to the possibility that "they" just might, on occasion, have a worthy insight, whether or not "they" acknowledge God as its source. It denies, in other words, that our merciful God often makes it possible for people with different motives and worldviews to agree at a practical level, something I discovered to my amazement when I worked with a diverse group of educators, parents, clergy, and school administrators to develop standards of conduct in our local school.

In the second place, the conspiracy mindset forgets that sin reaches everywhere, even to the "good guys." "We" are no more exempt from the influence of spiritual darkness than "they" are. History teaches us that yesterday's oppressed are often today's oppressors.

In the third place, the conspiracy mentality simplifies complex matters by pigeonholing people ("Well, blacks are like that, you know!" "Those liberals are baby killing socialists!" "The religious right are boneheaded selfish reactionaries!" "Women would never stand for this!"). Such sociological cloning overlooks the rich diversity among people and their opinions. It denies, in other words, the notion that each of us is distinct, "fearfully and wonderfully made" (Psalm 139:14).

Of course a ferocious and constant war rages. Scripture reminds us of this repeatedly (see Ephesians 6:12 and Revelation 12, especially verse 17). But according to the Bible this war is not essentially between the church and the state, or between the Christian and the government, or even between the opposing factions in the culture wars. Good and evil are at war, and both of these realities show up everywhere—in the church and in government; in Republicans, in Democrats, and in Independents; in gays and in straights; in Christians and in non-Christians.

A law professor in my church once gave me some thoughtful advice in the midst of a discussion on the abortion issue. He asked, "Have you ever considered calling up the local president of the abortion rights movement and having a 'nonpolitical' cup of coffee together? You could tell her that you are pro-life, but that your aim is not to argue. You want instead to listen and understand. She might be amazed to discover that you really care about the mothers involved in difficult pregnancies. Perhaps something positive might develop!" I had become so accustomed to the we/they approach that such a thought had never crossed my mind.

A pastor friend in North Carolina heard about this advice and took it to heart. He later wrote me:

> The Lord helped us to get a "Blue Moon Group" started down here. Each month now for nearly two years, I, along with one of my Associate Pastors, one of our elders, and one of our elders' wives (who is a nurse), get to meet over coffee and baked goods with the only doctor who performs abortions in this part of the state, her nurse practitioner, the Director of Planned Parenthood, and a local civil rights activist and community organizer. Along the way we have been able to bring into the group the Director of Catholic Social Services and now the Director of the local Pregnancy Support Services! All the major "players" are meeting each month to find common ground and to lessen the chances of violence in our community (the clinic has been bombed and the windows shot out in past years). Out of this the FemCare clinic (the abortion facility) is beginning to counsel some of their patients to meet with the Pregnancy Support Services or Catholic Social Services folks. They have even had a client call me for counsel before she had her abortion (she ended up keeping her baby!).

This is not the only example of such a development. James Hunter describes a number of cooperative agreements between pro-lifers and pro-choicers. One of them, which exists between Reproductive Health Services (RHS) of St. Louis and Missouri Citizens for Life, grew out of the RHS director's invitation to the chief pro-life attorney to look for common ground together:

> As reported in the *New York Times*, "...when a pregnant 10-year-old came to the abortion clinic, but decided to carry her pregnancy to term, Jean Cavender, the clinic's director of public affairs and a participant in the common-ground talks, called Ms. Wagner [of Missouri Citizens for Life] for help. She told Ms. Wagner that the girl needed to stay in bed because the pregnancy was medically complicated but that because her mother worked there was no one to care for her during the day. Ms. Wagner then raised enough money in anti-abortion circles to pay for an attendant and found a woman willing to go into the girl's dangerous drug-infested neighborhood. The baby was later put up for adoption."[49]

Who knows what good might come out of a concerted effort to cooperate like this?

Learning from George Washington

George Washington effectively brought people together. The delegates who gathered in Philadelphia in the sweltering summer of 1787 for what became the Constitutional Convention had many and profound differences of opinion on the ordering of the new nation. The miraculous consensus that emerged owed at least as much to informal tavern talk as to formal public debate. Washington, who was silent in the latter, played a key role in the former. A biographer noted:

> At the convivial gatherings, Washington was endlessly present, dining at one place, having supper at another, chatting between the acts of plays. He sought always to bring diverse points of view into the open and then together. History will never be able to assess the

extent of the contribution Washington made through such personal contacts, but it was surely great...He had, to a superlative degree, the gift for finding beneath controversy common ground.[50]

Like our first President, we should seek to be masters of cooperation, whether in public life or in church. Without compromising our principles, we should always be on the lookout for common cause. We should pursue that common cause humbly, knowing that both our wisdom and our goodness must grow. We should seek to persuade rather than coerce, knowing that the former engages people in a more socially healthy search for common ground than does the latter. The principle of cooperation guides, in other words, the *tone* of our political and social involvement, a critical dimension to public life that we unfortunately do not consider enough.

Washington's cooperative spirit thrived on his genuine humility, the preeminent grace that seems to have made him, in James Flexner's terms, "the indispensable man." In many of the crucial debates of his day, notably those in 1787 and 1788 over the ratification of the Constitution, he chose to remain silent, lest his immense prestige interfere with the experiment in self-governance at its start: "Washington became passionately eager to have the Constitution ratified...As Washington watched [the state delegations debating], he again and again strained as on a leash to interfere. However, he had resolved to take no part in the debate."[51] When he did speak, his humble statesmanship moved and united people remarkably.

If we truly believe ourselves to be sinners, we will be the first to admit that we may be wrong. We will listen carefully and accuse rarely. We will build community rather than tear it down. We are told that Washington delivered his inaugural address "with trembling voice and trembling hands" and with an aspect that was "grave almost to sadness," qualities that deeply affected contemporary orators like Fisher Ames: "It seemed to me an allegory in which virtue was personified, and addressing those whom she would make her votaries. Her power over the heart was never greater."[52]

We must not forget what Washington understood and demonstrated so well: political solutions are rarely easy or obvious in our fallen world. To find them we must learn to work together humbly in common cause, both outside the church and within it. The conspiracy mentality calls for an altogether different spirit, a mean and distrustful one. Such a spirit profoundly undermines the capacity for communication, constructive disagreement, and workable compromise, civic graces without which common cause is impossible.

We call ourselves sinners saved by grace, which means that we claim to have been humbled by the undeserved love of God. If we mean what we say, the conspiracy mentality will be alien to us. Grateful for God's mercy and alert to our own weakness, we will be slow to accuse and swift to build.

The Third Approach: Be Yourself Today

In *Kingdoms in Conflict* Charles Colson introduces us to Jack Eckerd and Trevor Ferrell, the former the wealthy founder of a drugstore chain, the latter an eleven-year-old boy.[53] In 1983 Jack Eckerd went after pornographic magazines, pulling them from the seventeen hundred drugstores bearing his name despite the financial risk, and urging other executives to follow suit. Eventually Revco, People's, Rite Aid, Dart Drug, High's Dairy Stores, and 7-Eleven did the same, largely through the initiative of one man who took to heart the public responsibility that attended the power providentially given him.

In December of the same year that Jack Eckerd began his fight, Trevor Ferrell persuaded his parents to drive him into inner-city Philadelphia so that he could bring a blanket to a homeless person. That first visit led to many more and a change not only in the Ferrell household but also in their church and their community as more and more became involved in "Trevor's Campaign." When asked by the media to explain his involvement, Trevor answered simply, "It's Jesus inside of me that makes me want to do this."[54]

Jack Eckerd and Trevor Ferrell were two very different people—one a wealthy businessman with a high degree of public clout, the other a boy with hardly any. What united them is the choice each made to use his gifts and opportunities to bring the reign of Christ to bear upon his particular world.

No two of us are alike. Our gifts, callings, and opportunities all differ. No two of us have the same amount or type of public clout, and therefore our activism as citizens will be splendidly diverse. This variation exists not only between people but also within the life span of each person. Mr. Eckerd probably had less clout in retirement than in he did in 1983 when he began his campaign against pornography. Trevor's public influence has no doubt also changed since 1983—possibly decreasing in some ways (he is no longer a media darling) and increasing in others. Think of the variation in Jesus' influence. In the early stages of his public ministry he was so popular that the masses tried to force him to be king. At the end he was rejected and alone. And there will come a day when "every knee should bow, in heaven and on earth and under the earth, and every tongue acknowledge that Jesus Christ is Lord" (Philippians 2:10–11). In his final role we can expect that Jesus will act as he did in his former roles—obediently and trustingly in accordance with the opportunities that are providentially his. Herein lies a lesson for us. Like our Lord, all of us need to discern our present and unique public calling, however small or great, and pursue it faithfully.

Finding Your Public Calling

How do you do this? First, assume that you have a public calling (we are all called to be salt and light). Second, ask yourself, *What issues or matters in public life get my attention? What do I care about?* Third, consider your circumstances by asking, *What opportunities has God set before me in the areas where I have some interest?* Fourth, do something. Take up one of the opportunities you have just discerned. God cannot steer a boat that isn't moving. He defines and modifies our calling as we act.

When I agreed to serve on the goal writing committee in our school district, I did so because I sensed a call to participate. By this I do not mean that God spoke audibly to me (he did not). Nor do I mean that every circumstance in my life pointed in that direction (I was already busy in my church responsibilities and I had no expertise in educational philosophy). What I mean is that opportunity, need, and interest came together sufficiently to persuade me that I should say yes to the invitation. For one thing, I had always had an interest in young people. For another, I had been for some time working with area clergy and school officials to draft a document on religion in the public schools. I knew that God wanted me to be involved in some way in my local community, and this particular way seemed to make sense.

Do something, however small. And as you do, cut some slack to other believers, none of whom (even if they serve on the same committee!) will have the same role as yours.

Making It Personal

1. Read over the "Song of Mary" (Luke 1:46–55), the text of which appears at the head of this chapter. List the social changes that she celebrates in her song. What do her words tell us about the sorts of social changes that matter most to God? Why is this so? Try to imagine how Mary must have felt, given her social clout at the time, to be chosen for her particular task. What can you learn from Mary's attitude, action, and perspective as you face social and political problems that are too big for you to handle?

2. Pick a social issue that is important to you and develop a plan to address it using one or more of the "avenues for change" discussed in this chapter (feel free to think of others):

   "We can pray for change. We can talk up change, seeking to persuade by reasoned argument. Or we can live out change, seeking to demonstrate its wisdom by example. We can protest what we deem an unjust law, or seek to change it by legislative process. We can create the appetite for change through the arts (Billie Holiday's *Strange Fruit*, a haunting jazz number about lynching, stirred our national conscience). Or we can go after social change indirectly but most radically by throwing ourselves into evangelism. And we can work for change at a variety of different social levels, beginning with the smallest community (alone on our knees) and ranging upward from a conversation over coffee to a national debate."

3. The first approach to God-honoring activism is respect for people. Discuss ways to humanize your interaction with public officials—like police officers, department of motor vehicle people, senators, state assemblymen, school board members, and so forth. If you happen to be a public official, discuss ways to make your dealings with your constituency more human and more responsive, especially to the poor and the less powerful. Finally discuss ways in which you can humanize your interactions with fellow believers who differ from you politically.

4. The second approach is to look for ways to cooperate. This chapter describes three teachings that should enhance our spirit of cooperation: (a) common grace, (b) total depravity, and (c) creation in the image of God. What do these teachings mean and why do they motivate us to be more cooperative?

5. Think of a group whose social agenda really upsets you. Try to devise a plan for approaching that group peaceably and for cooperating with that group in some common endeavor.

6. The third approach is to be yourself—that is, do what's doable for you. Try to define your public calling. As you do so be sure to ask for input from friends (we are always blind to certain things about ourselves). The following advice from the chapter should prove helpful:

"First, assume that you have a public calling (we are all called to be salt and light). Second, ask yourself, *What issues or matters in public life get my attention? What do I care about?* Third, consider your circumstances by asking, *What opportunities has God set before me in the areas where I have some interest?* Fourth, do something. Take up one of the opportunities you have just discerned."

If I have walked with falsehood…or if my hands have been defiled, then may others eat what I have sown, and may my crops be uprooted. If my heart has been enticed by a woman, or if I have lurked at my neighbor's door, then may my wife grind another man's grain, and may other men sleep with her…If I have denied justice to any of my servants, whether male or female, when they had a grievance against me…If I have denied the desires of the poor or…the widow…if I have kept my bread to myself…if I have seen anyone perishing for lack of clothing…if I have raised my hand against the fatherless, knowing that I had influence in court…then let my arm fall from the shoulder…For I dreaded destruction from God, and for fear of his splendor I could not do such things. If I have put my trust in gold…if I have regarded the sun in its radiance…so that my heart was secretly enticed… then these also would be sins to be judged, for I would have been unfaithful to God on high. If I have rejoiced at my enemy's misfortune…if I have concealed my sin as people do, by hiding my guilt in my heart…if my land cries out against me…if I have devoured its yield without payment or broken the spirit of its tenants, then let briers come up instead of wheat and stinkweed instead of barley. (Job 31:5–40)

Chapter 9

TWO MORE APPROACHES: PRESSING ON AND KEEPING IT SIMPLE

In June 1939 German pastor Dietrich Bonhoeffer sailed to America to teach and wait out the war that had erupted in his homeland. But before long he found that his conscience would not permit him to remain in safety. Upon leaving for home less than a month later he wrote to Reinhold Niebuhr: "I have made a mistake in coming to America. I must live through this difficult period of our national history with the Christian people of Germany. I will have no right to participate in the reconstruction of Christian life in Germany after the war if I do not share the trials of this time with my people."[55] Arrested in 1943 for his role in the German resistance, Bonhoeffer was hanged on April 9, 1945, one week before the allies liberated his prison.

When Martin Luther King Jr. set out to bring an end to segregation and voting injustice in Alabama and Mississippi, he faced enormous opposition. Fellow clergy spoke out against him. From time to time, even close friends and allies sought to dissuade him. His house was bombed and close friends were killed. In the end he lost his own life. But these odds did not deter him from either goal or method.

Both Bonhoeffer and King were men of integrity. This does not mean that they were flawless (none of us is). Nor does it mean that their choices were always wise or perfect (whose are?). Rather it means that they were servants of the heavenly King who understood that pleasing him was more important than being safe or successful. It also means that they resisted today's commonplace tendency to separate private living from public living. They sought to live as those whose lives in their entirety (not just the "spiritual" side) belonged to Christ. It was, in fact, their refusal to keep their faith private that got them into trouble.

Bonhoeffer and King could have traced their spiritual descent from Job. That ancient figure, whose final cry of innocence appears in partial form at the head of this chapter, seems to have known nothing of our fashionable modern distinction between public and private behavior. In one breath he spoke of sexual purity, ecological responsibility, undivided worship, justice in the courtroom, honesty in the marketplace, care for the poor, and guileless speech. Pursuing social justice and having a good devotional life carried equal weight for him because his life as a whole belonged to the God of all things.

So must it be with us. When our devotional life dries up, we nevertheless press on—because we know that it is good and healthy to pursue the Lord in prayer and meditation. Similarly, when our efforts to make society a better place encounter opposition, we nevertheless keep at it, because we know that our Lord values justice and human love as much as he values prayer.

Press On (the Fourth Approach)

We must choose to do what is right simply because it is right, and not because it is always easy, popular, successful, or even (in extreme cases) lawful. Jesus encourages us in this by his example. Though his public ministry began strongly, it ended in disaster from a worldly perspective. The adoring crowds deserted him and eventually turned upon him.

Jesus "failed" because he would not compromise. Those who sought to trap him with the question on taxation spoke truly when they said, "Teacher, we know that you are a man of integrity. You aren't swayed by others, because you pay no attention to who they are" (Mark 12:14). Jesus repeatedly confronted his followers with disturbing truths about themselves. He told them to forsake all in following him. He disappointed the crowds by refusing to allow them to make him king, for he knew that this was not God's plan. He made a shambles of the temple courts because the commercialism there infuriated his Father. He exposed the greed, hypocrisy, and emptiness of the religious leaders. When on trial for his life, he told the truth about himself, even though he knew it would enrage his accusers and confirm them in their resolve to kill him. Such words and deeds were unpopular, but this made no difference to Jesus, since truth demanded that he say and do them.

The apostles followed in their Master's footsteps. Beaten and jailed for preaching Christ and threatened with death if they continued, Peter and the others answered the authorities, "We must obey God rather than human beings!" (Acts 5:29; see verses 27–33). No doubt Peter said this respectfully, for we know that he saw all authority as coming from God. Nevertheless, with simple boldness and for the sake of the truth, he refused to obey. In this instance, giving God his due meant denying what "Caesar" demanded.

Such integrity can cost us our lives, as it did King and Bonhoeffer. It can land us in jail, as happened to many who chose to involve themselves in Operation Rescue. It may lose us some friends as my wife experienced when she politely refused to pay a friend "off the books" for housecleaning. On rare occasions "pressing on" makes public heroes of us, as it did Trevor Ferrell, the boy mentioned in the last chapter who handed out blankets to the homeless. Most of the time, however, we find it impossible to measure its impact. Often God is the only one who sees.

Pressing On and Civil Disobedience

In the Long Island town where I once lived, two historic churches face each other across the village green—Caroline Church of Brookhaven (Episcopal) and Setauket Presbyterian Church. A little over two hundred years ago, the Presbyterians watched with dismay as the occupying British troops turned their building into a stable for their horses while they worshiped across the green at Caroline. Such desecration occurred because Episcopalians tended to be loyal to the British crown and Presbyterians tended not to be. Two historic lessons present themselves: Christians have chosen to take up arms against the authorities that govern them, and Christians have had differing opinions on when they may take such action.

May the "pressing on" approach to activism ever lead to civil disobedience? Many Christians believe so. The apostle Peter tells us to respect emperors and governors because they "are sent by [God] to punish those who do wrong and to commend those who do right" (1 Peter 2:13–14). Implied in this high moral calling are grounds, many believe, not only for critique but also for disobedience. When a government flagrantly violates God's description of its calling—when a government exalts evil and punishes good—grounds for disobedience are seen to exist.

In the last one hundred years we have witnessed apartheid and the Holocaust (coming from the political Right) and the Soviet Gulag resettlement camps (coming from the Left). We have seen Austria, Czechoslovakia, Afghanistan, Chile, and many other nations overrun or "destabilized" by foreign countries. We have heard of Christian children being forcibly removed from their homes and brought up in state-run institutions. We have had our fill of regimes (communist and fascist) that rewarded people for publicly lying and for denouncing their families, friends, and neighbors. We have been troubled by stories of people who have been punished by their governments for seeking to help fellow citizens escape oppression.

By God's grace most modern Americans have not had to live directly under such oppression. But what of believers in other countries, or believers at earlier times in our own history? What about blacks in our own time? Bonhoeffer joined the plot to kill Hitler. In 1856 John Brown killed four pro-slavery settlers in his efforts to keep slavery out of Kansas. Harriet Tubman repeatedly broke the law in helping runaway slaves escape to the north, and the only reason she never used the pistol she packed seems to be that no one ever caught her. Martin Luther King Jr. acted in defiance of numerous court orders. Some Christians trespass on the grounds of abortion clinics in their protest against abortion laws.

Members of Setauket Presbyterian Church, many of whom no doubt loved the Scriptures, took up arms against King George.

Pressing On: Violent and Nonviolent Resistance

Civil disobedience can, of course, take many forms. It can be violent and nonviolent. Martin Luther King Jr. practiced the latter with great effect. To those who complained that his approach was too passive, King distinguished sharply between "nonresistance to evil" and "nonviolent resistance," advocating the latter and contending that it can in fact be very aggressive and deliberate.

On December 1, 1955, Mrs. Rosa Parks, a black woman, refused to surrender her seat to a white man who boarded the bus she was riding on. By her act she broke the Montgomery, Alabama, law. Her arrest prompted King and others to call for further resistance through a boycott of the city bus system in protest. So effective was the boycott that it nearly bankrupted the bus company. King and many others were arrested, and charged with violating anti-boycott law. Following his conviction on March 22, 1956, King wrote:

> Ordinarily, a person leaving a courtroom with a conviction behind him would wear a somber face. But I left with a smile. I knew that I was a convicted criminal, but I was proud of my crime. It was the crime of joining my people in a nonviolent protest against injustice. It was the crime of seeking to instill within my people a sense of dignity and self-respect. It was the crime of desiring for my people the unalienable (sic) rights of life, liberty, and the pursuit of happiness. It was above all the crime of seeking to convince my people that non-cooperation with evil is as much a moral duty as is cooperation with good.[56]

Throughout those months, even when his home was bombed, King acted and counseled his many followers to act without violence. His cause and his method captured the attention of the nation, and on November 13, nearly a year after Rosa Parks refused to leave her seat, the United States Supreme Court declared Montgomery's laws unconstitutional.

Violent Resistance?

Nonviolent resistance appeals to many Christians. But what about violent resistance? May a Christian ever protest injustice with force? If so, under what circumstances? How, for example, do we distinguish between the violence of John Brown and the (intended) violence of Dietrich Bonhoeffer? What is the difference between bombing an abortion clinic in 1997 (or protesting violently during a Black Lives Matter rally in 2018) and firing at British soldiers in 1776?

The answers to these questions are difficult and beyond the scope of this book. What we can say is that some thoughtful Christians have found grounds for violent resistance. They have found it morally conceivable that one may need to use violence to resist a greater violence, as did some ethnic Albanians living in Kosovo in 1999 when their nation's police burned their homes and murdered their kinfolk.

Violent resistance may be justifiable, but those who choose it must do so with great reluctance, knowing that even bad governments exist by God's mercy to restrain the human race's natural tendency towards anarchy. If they ever choose violence, they should have first exhausted every other option, because they know that violence nearly always begets violence. They should recall the bloodbaths following the French and Russian revolutions, acknowledging that the overthrow of evil regimes has often opened the way to much worse ones. And they should repudiate the arrogance of claiming that they are God's holy warriors bringing in the kingdom of God through their acts of violence. In this regard Bonhoeffer seems to have little in common with the self-styled prophet John Brown.

Integrity must characterize our public life. Results, publicity, our own safety, and peace must never be our primary concern but must rather be left in the hands of the one who has called us to leave all and follow him.

Keep It Simple (The Fifth Approach)

Where do we begin? So many things cry out for attention that we can easily become overwhelmed. We resist being daunted by committing ourselves to the principle of simplicity. We will start by doing what is obvious and simple, rather than with what is cosmic and subtle. "How do you eat an elephant?" asks the sage. His answer: "One bite at a time!"

In the parable of the good Samaritan Jesus taught that our neighbor, the proper object of our care, is anyone in need whom God has placed providentially at our feet. Care for that wounded man may have been inconvenient (there were other important things to do), socially unacceptable (Samaritans and Jews hated each other), and even dangerous (bandits were known to lure victims by feigning injury on the Jericho road). But it was obvious and doable. Simplicity counsels us, "Before you rush off to develop a program that will provide better care for wounded travelers, or that will increase security on the Jericho road, take care of this particular man. See where that takes you."

Some good friends of mine have taken a series of pregnant teenagers into their home. They have, in other words, addressed the abortion issue with simplicity, one child and one mother at a time. This is not to say that they have avoided other involvements. The principle of simplicity advises us on where to *begin* addressing a matter of public concern.

Nor is it to suggest that the obvious and the doable will be the same on a given issue for every person. Jack Eckerd's first step in fighting pornography might differ dramatically from that of a Christian clerk in one of his stores or a father who often shops there.

Two Stories

Because a church in which I once served is in a fairly affluent section of Long Island, we did not have access to homeless people unless we went in search of them. For this reason it came as something of a surprise to us when Dennis, rather "ripe" from too much alcohol and too little soap, joined us one Sunday morning for worship. Only mildly distracting during the first part of worship, he began crying out incoherently during the sermon. Uncertain of exactly how to respond, I was relieved when two men and a woman arose from their seats and quietly removed the troubled man. I later learned that they had acted with no clear idea of what to do once they had removed Dennis; they had simply had a willingness to help as the Lord gave wisdom.

What began with the simple decision to do the obvious thing evolved, for one of the men, into something greater. Tim made friends with Dennis. He found him a place to live and over the next year saw him through both a detox and a literacy program. In the process our church came to know a number of homeless people and became involved in a soup kitchen ministry. Perhaps even more will come of Tim's decision to do the obvious thing. Who knows? This story did not draw media attention—it simply is not big enough. But I am convinced that it drew God's attention, for this is the way he usually advances his kingdom in the life of a nation.

A bigger and better known story features Barbara Vogel's fifth grade students at Highland Community School in Aurora, Colorado. In February 1998 she read them a newspaper article about the thriving and brutal slavery industry in Sudan. The students learned that that country's Islamic government was making war upon its own people, sanctioning raids on the non-Islamic Dinka villages to the south. The victorious raiders were routinely carrying off women and children and selling them into slavery. So moved were Barbara Vogel's students that they researched the problem on the Internet to see if they could do anything about it. They discovered Christian Solidarity International (CSI), a Swiss organization that buys Sudanese slaves their freedom for about fifty dollars. Armed with this information, they undertook a campaign aimed at freeing Sudanese slaves, one at a time. According to a magazine report,

> They collected allowance money, organized lemonade-stand sales, and sold used toys to raise money. After publicity on national television shows, the fifth graders, along with Vogel's new fourth-grade class last fall, began receiving individual and corporate donations from around the country. With every $50 raised, the students added a new brown-paper cutout of a freed slave to the classroom wall.[57]

In seventeen months Vogel's young people raised fifty thousand dollars and fired a nationwide movement that enabled CSI to redeem thousands. The striking thing about this remarkable effort is that it began so simply. A handful of students discovered a need to which they could relate (many slaves are the same age as their liberators), and they took steps to do what they could. Mother Teresa's wise and powerful words, "Do small things with great love," bedeck one of Barbara Vogel's classroom walls. They remind us that there is always something we can do to make this world a better place. (*Note:* It is with great sadness and frustration that supporters of this initiative heard of slave dealers re-enslaving liberated children so that they could "make" even more money from re-redemptions. In our deeply fallen world, great evil can arise out of great kindness. This terrible fact should make us wise in our efforts, but it should not make us so cynical that we stop caring. Christ promises to make all things right, and we press on as best we can with hope, knowing that he will.)

Pulling It All Together: Incarnational Living

We have been talking about public discipleship throughout this book—about following Jesus into the world, both as individuals and as the people of God. We can summarize all that we have been saying with Jesus' own words: "Whoever wants to be my disciple must deny themselves and take up their cross and follow me" (Matthew 16:24). We follow Jesus not simply by promoting what he says but by embracing his way of doing things—his *modus operandi*. We choose self-denial and, if necessary, suffering, all for love's sake.

A single word that describes Jesus' *modus operandi* is incarnation. He let go of his glory, rights, privileges, and freedoms as the eternal Son in order to join us fully in our human condition and to serve us there. But he did so without taking on our values. In other words, he always took his orders from outside the world he had entered. And for that reason he never quite fit in and in the end suffered death at the hands of those he came to serve. When Jesus tells us to follow him he means for us to follow this same pattern. We fully enter the world as its friends while taking our orders from outside. If that means we suffer, then so be it.

Notice how so much of what we have been discussing gathers around this pattern. When like Jesus we engage the world as its servants, we are less apt either to demonize it or abandon it (chapter 1). When we relate to one another (in the church) as servants, we listen harder and are less apt to grow angry over politics (chapter 2). When we really take our orders from outside, trusting God to fix the world in his own time and way, we panic less (chapter 1), pray more (chapter 3), seek more diligently to conduct our public lives in a manner that is above reproach (chapter 4), press past what is merely legal in search of what is truly good (chapter 6), and think more carefully and behave more graciously as we press for change (chapter 7).

Think of the five approaches to change we have just discussed (chapters 8 and 9). They too cluster around the pattern of Jesus' incarnation. We find the foundation for *respect* and *cooperation* in our Lord's choice to enter our world as our friend, committed to winning us over from the inside, not by force, but by love and persuasion. He chose not to stand at the outskirts of our world, lobbing heavenly slogans at us like mortar rounds from the other side of the barricade. Instead, he lived alongside us, entering our story, facing our trials, enduring our sufferings, speaking our language. We find as well the foundation for *diversity*. Though Jesus was the Creator and Sustainer of all, he did not travel the world, solving every problem. He bloomed where he was planted, in Israel and mostly among fellow Jews, leaving the final and comprehensive solution in his Father's hands. Think also of *simplicity*. Though Jesus was the promised Messiah, he steadfastly chose service over power, refusing to seize the latter, even though it was his right, from the moment that Satan offered it to him in the wilderness to the moment of his arrest when he could have called angel legions to his defense. He left the vindication of his life and work in the Father's hands and timing. Think finally of *integrity*. As Jesus walked among us he took his orders from outside, obeying those orders faithfully to the end—regardless of the results, even if obedience meant failure (humanly speaking), humiliation and death.

Jesus' manner of engaging the world gives us a mandate for involvement. But it also reins in the foolish triumphalism that makes us impatient with our neighbors and with one another. To choose incarnation is to choose faithfulness and service over outcomes, leaving the latter in God's hands. We can expect to be resisted, we can even expect to suffer—for to love the world as Jesus did means, at heart, taking up a cross—not winning an argument or an election. Nevertheless our efforts have value and lasting effect: insofar as we are obedient, wise, and loving in our public lives, God notes our efforts, rejoices over them, and values them as tokens of what is to be when his Son returns to make all things right. What is more, in some mysterious way, he causes them to last, promising that our "labor in the Lord is not in vain" (1 Corinthians 15:58).

Postscript

My church once sent me to Bangladesh to visit a number of the missionaries we support. India's eastern neighbor is an extremely poor Islamic country living constantly on the edge of political and economic disaster. In its brief history the country has experienced a series of severe famines and has rarely seen a change in political leadership without bloodshed. The believers there comprise less than one percent of the population. Full of remarkable faith and vitality, they have next to no influence politically and socially.

Within a week of my return from Bangladesh, I attended a New York Rangers ice hockey game at Madison Square Garden with our son. When we rose to sing the national anthem I was moved as I had never before been, thanks to my Bangladesh experience. For many in the stands that night, that song seemed to mean little more than a signal that the game was about to start. For me it was a reminder of the privilege and responsibility I possess as an American believer. Because I am an American, I belong to a political tradition that guarantees my freedom to assemble, to worship, and to speak and act according to conscience—in short to be public about my faith. Because I am a Christian I have a responsibility to make the most of that tradition, for Christ has placed me in it.

But I have yet another, and higher, responsibility. And that responsibility is to fulfill my public calling in a manner that reveals Christ and builds his church. It is said that a woman approached Benjamin Franklin following the long session that produced the Constitution of the United States and asked him,

"Sir, what is it going to be? A monarchy or a republic?" Franklin responded, "Madam, it is going to be a republic, *if* we can keep it." It is a good thing to heed Franklin's warning—to love our country and work hard to preserve her great freedoms. But it is an even better thing to preserve and build the church.

Never forget that the only social institution that will survive the fires at the end of history is the church—America will cease to be, along with the Republican Party, the Democratic Party, the NRA, and the ACLU. And the church will survive, not on the margins of society, but at its center. We will *be* the society. Our task now is to prove that this is so not simply by the *fact* of our engagement with the world but by the *quality* of it, and, above all, by the quality of our life together. We must demonstrate the winsome power of Christ to break down the walls that divide us—including the political walls. God help us. Much is at stake.

Making It Personal

1. Read Job's far-ranging testimony to his innocence at the head of this chapter, and list fully the different areas of life that he covers. Inventory your own life in the light of Job's list. Are there any areas that need scrutiny?

2. Like his hero Gandhi, Martin Luther King Jr. practiced nonviolent resistance. Discuss the following statement, made by King immediately following a criminal conviction:

   > Ordinarily, a person leaving a courtroom with a conviction behind him would wear a somber face. But I left with a smile. I knew that I was a convicted criminal, but I was proud of my crime. It was the crime of joining my people in a nonviolent protest against injustice. It was the crime of seeking to instill within my people a sense of dignity and self-respect. It was the crime of desiring for my people the unalienable (sic) rights of life, liberty, and the pursuit of happiness. It was above all the crime of seeking to convince my people that non-cooperation with evil is as much a moral duty as is cooperation with good.

3. Why were King and Gandhi successful? Share and discuss examples of nonviolent resistance you have witnessed or participated in. Are there any present-day injustices that you believe call for nonviolent resistance?

4. What circumstances, if any, would prompt you to resist United States authority violently? What nonviolent means of resistance would you have exhausted first? What form would your violent resistance take? What greater violence and injustice might your violence provoke?

5. The principle of simplicity calls us to change our world by behaving as the good Samaritan behaved, by doing whatever is obvious and doable. Share examples of this sort of action that you have seen or participated in. Is there anything obvious and doable that you or a group you are a part of can undertake?

6. Spend some time in prayer. Thank God for the many social and political freedoms you enjoy. Ask God for the sort of love, strength, perseverance, and wisdom that will enable you to make your community, your church, and your country a better place. Pray especially for the unity of the church and for wisdom on how you can best contribute to it.

Put to death, therefore, whatever belongs to your earthly nature: sexual immorality, impurity, lust, evil desires and greed, which is idolatry. Because of these, the wrath of God is coming. You used to walk in these ways, in the life you once lived. But now you must rid yourselves of all such things as these: anger, rage, malice, slander, and filthy language from your lips. Do not lie to each other, since you have taken off your old self with its practices and have put on the new self, which is being renewed in knowledge in the image of its Creator. Here there is no Greek or Jew, circumcised or uncircumcised, barbarian, Scythian, slave or free, but Christ is all, and is in all. Therefore, as God's chosen people, holy and dearly loved, clothe yourselves with compassion, kindness, humility, gentleness and patience. Bear with each other and forgive whatever grievances you may have against one another. Forgive as the Lord forgave you. And over all these virtues put on love, which binds them all together in perfect unity. Let the peace of Christ rule in your hearts, since as members of one body you were called to peace. And be thankful. Let the word of Christ dwell in you richly as you teach and admonish one another with all wisdom, and as you sing psalms, hymns and spiritual songs with gratitude in your hearts to God. And whatever you do, whether in word or deed, do it all in the name of the Lord Jesus, giving thanks to God the Father through him. (Colossians 3:5-17)

Chapter 10

TALKING ABOUT POLITICS AT CHURCH

In the Introduction of this book we describe a church-wide forum we held on faith and politics prior to the 2016 election followed by two responses from parishioners who attended. Here are some additional responses to that event.

- The panel discussion we had at our church…was engaging, relatable, civilized and encouraging. It proved that those who hold the same basic values dear but choose differing means of advancing their causes can have challenging and purposeful conversation. ("Christine"--a Christian counselor)

- I felt a sense of liberation from the fear of being able to have an open discussion about topics that can often be divisive within the church… I was heartened by the encouragement to struggle over how my faith might influence my political views, to discover that others struggle to do the same thing, and that it can be a lonely journey. I'm hopeful that this discussion will continue even beyond the election, and that the church can unite to bring peace and reconciliation to a country that is at the moment caught in despair, fear, and frustration. ("Sally": A public school teacher)

- The workshop was a wonderful opportunity to honestly and respectfully discuss political issues often avoided in church social circles... It was a powerful example of church unity and challenged me to more actively build this unity within the broader universal church. ("George": A graduate student at Columbia Business School)

The aim of this final chapter is to help you build a church culture in which forums and responses like this can happen.

Cultivating a peaceable culture in church

First I will need to acknowledge that such a culture has to be cultivated. It does not spring up overnight. We had many years prior developed and articulated a philosophy of our church's engagement with culture (see Appendix C at the end of the book). Building on that philosophy, we had held similar forums prior to the national elections in 2008 and 2012, and in anticipation of each I had preached a series of sermons on the church and politics. In each case we had chosen the panel participants with great care. They had in every case been people of character and grace, and in no case had they been church officers (we bent over backwards to make sure that church power was never an ingredient in the mix). In every case we had vetted what each panelist was going to say, and in every case the panelists had, prior to the meeting, shared with each other what they were going to say and had prayed together.

To cultivate such a culture we have found that the preaching and public prayer ministry must be done with care and nuance, so as not to give the impression that there is a "Christian" angle on a particular candidate or election outcome. As to the preaching, we have chosen not to preach on politics immediately before a national election when everybody is wound up. That can be a little like asking teenagers to download and listen to a talk on sexual ethics when they are by themselves holding hands on a park bench on a warm summer evening. We have sought to weave talk about responsible social and political involvement into the culture and teaching of the church all the time.

Some distinctions that can help

What follows are some of the distinctions that we have found helpful for reducing political heat at church as we have framed teaching, preaching, and public prayer. Found in various places through this book, I will summarize them here.

The distinction between public engagement narrowly and broadly defined
First there is the distinction between public engagement narrowly defined and public engagement broadly defined.

The first of these is power politics—getting certain people into office and certain policies and laws implemented. Power politics is limited, imprecise, and coercive. Voting, for example, is a blunt instrument: a single pull of a lever endorses a whole host of things. Party platforms, for another example, are never entirely what we want. Politicians are flawed, quickly out of office, and possess limited power even when they are in office. Laws can never cover every contingency. For all these reasons banking on power politics is both irritating and frustrating, a recipe for divisiveness in church.

Public engagement broadly defined (we can call it public influence) is very different. It includes all sorts of undertakings which are open to all sorts of people. We can pray down God's kingdom. We can make public goodness attractive by our example. We can advocate for the good, the true, and the beautiful through the arts. We can tell good stories through journalism, books, and screen plays. We can talk with "the opposition" over a non-politicized cup of coffee.

No one person can do all these things: we are differently gifted. But everybody can do something (praying comes to mind), and with changes in our seasons of life and opportunity many of us can move from one realm of influence to another. Reminding one another of the nearly limitless possibilities for public influence, and encouraging one another to become involved somehow in this broader undertaking, dramatically reduces the frustration that so often accompanies the more narrowly construed view of social and political engagement. And when we reduce frustration, we also reduce anger.

The distinction between theocracy and influence

A second distinction that can cultivate a more peaceable culture at church is between the theocrat in each of us and the influencer in each of us. We can help one another to identify and distance ourselves from the first of these. The "theocrat within" tends to identify a particular group or strategy with God and his strategy. His aim is to see that group or strategy win, and, because winning is so important, he will, unless he is vigilant, tend to permit the ends to justify the means. Motives and methods will play second fiddle to advancing what he believes God wants. The theocrat in us tends not to care as much as he should about getting the facts right and listening carefully and respectfully to the "opposition's" point of view.

The "influencer" within each of us is a different sort of animal, and contributes to a more peaceable church. She doesn't deny theocracy (Jesus is the King and he aims to overthrow everything that stands opposed to his Father's will), but she keeps reminding herself that the sword of Jesus issues from his mouth and not his hand (see the vision of Jesus in Revelation 1). Persuasion, rather than force, is her King's preferred method for advancing his agenda. He aims to rule our hearts, rather than to force our conformity. He seeks only volunteers in his army. Because of her love for Jesus' aims and methods, the "influencer within" will seek patiently to nudge the culture (and church friends) in the right direction by argument and example, resorting to law only as a last resort. She doesn't have to win. She chooses instead to serve. She sees the "opposition party" (even, and especially, at church) as her friends and does all that she can to come alongside them so that she can hear them out and serve their aims wherever she can find common cause. Because winning is not her aim, she is not crushed or infuriated by losing. She never manipulates. What drives her is faithfulness rather than results: if something wonderful and culture changing (or church-changing) catches on because of her efforts, great; if instead nothing changes and she suffers for her faithfulness, that's OK too. Outcomes are Jesus' business, not hers.

Imagine a church filled with people who permit the "influencer within" to triumph over the "theocrat within". That church will be an honest place (efforts to persuade will take place). But it will also be a safe and happy place—a social surprise to friends and neighbors.

The distinction between moral principles and political strategies

Perhaps the most important and helpful "heat-reducing" distinction is between moral principles and political strategies. Moral principles are the high commands of God: love God with all you've got and love your neighbor as yourself. Faithful church leaders will never dance around these high commands, even if it costs them to promote them.

Political strategies (which we sometimes confuse with moral principles—with angry results) are a different animal. They are fallible human efforts to nudge the culture in the direction of greater conformity to moral principles. Faithful church leaders, when it comes to strategies, will protect the consciences of their people so that no one in the church is made to feel like a second class citizen over them. You will find illustrations of this distinction at work earlier in the book.

The "principle/strategy" distinction is not a cure all. Sometimes we will disagree over which moral principles apply to a particular issue. Sometimes we will discover what seem to be conflicting moral principles, or we will disagree over which moral principles should be more decisive when we are deciding which party platform to endorse when we vote. And sometimes we will disagree with each other on how to interpret a particular text (say, "subdue the earth" or "you shall not kill"). Nevertheless keeping this distinction in mind can be an enormous help as we try to navigate our political differences.

You can perhaps see why this is so. When we identify a political strategy with a God-given moral principle, there can be no room for discussion. The strategy becomes a litmus test for fellowship. Conversations end. Fellowship becomes hollow and mistrustful. Churches split. But when we choose not to identify a political strategy this way, we are less apt to see the believer with the opposing view as the enemy of God, and therefore as our enemy in some essential way. With less at stake, we find that we can keep talking and listening. We may even find, as we talk and listen, that surprising solutions to difficult issues begin to arise. In any event, we find that we can agree to disagree if necessary and we can still have the Lord's Supper together. We can, in short, be a social surprise to our friends and neighbors.

Framing and leading public prayers

Church people (leaders especially) can find it difficult knowing how to pray publicly about politics. We must do this: the world needs the church's prayers and Jesus commands them. But how do we do it? How, we wonder, can we say something substantive without running the risk of infuriating certain people in the pews and undermining the unity of the church? Here are some suggestions, first regarding tone and then regarding content.

Two suggestions regarding tone

First, when we rise to pray for our country we have good cause to do so with humility. The opening of Nehemiah's prayer over Israel following her return from exile instructs us:

> *Then I said: "O LORD, God of heaven, the great and awesome God, who keeps his covenant of love with those who love him and obey his commands, [6] let your ear be attentive and your eyes open to hear the prayer your servant is praying before you day and night for your servants, the people of Israel. I confess the sins we Israelites, including myself and my father's house, have committed against you. [7] We have acted very wickedly toward you. We have not obeyed the commands, decrees and laws you gave your servant Moses. (Nehemiah 1:5-7)*

Nehemiah opens his appeal confessing two things: God's faithfulness and Israel's lack of it. Notably he includes himself in Israel's failure: "... *[I] and my father's house have [sinned] against you.*"

As we prepare to pray publicly we would be wise to remind ourselves that the United States is "our" country, not "their" country. We may not like a particular leader or set of leaders, or we may take deep exception to a particular law or policy; but we belong to this country and not to some other. Over John the Baptist's objections, Jesus chose, though innocent, to identify with Israel's sins through baptism. We too can identify with the sins of our country, all the more so since we cannot claim to be innocent. Even if we didn't vote for the "bad guys", we are in one way or another always complicit in what is wrong, by neglect and indifference if nothing else. Knowing this can help wean us from a critical and judgmental spirit as we pray.

A helpful and humbling "pre-prayer" exercise is to think of public figures whom we dislike as mirrors in which we get to view ourselves. If, for example, a civic leader infuriates us for habitually "spinning" facts to his advantage, we would be wise to ask a friend help us identify how we do the same sort of thing. Seeing our complicity in similar behavior won't necessarily keep us from praying for change in a public figure, but it will likely take the huffiness out of us as we do so. It will also likely broaden our praying against "spin" in public life so that we won't make the mistake (infuriating to some of our hearers) of assuming that this particular figure has cornered the market on this particular public sin.

Here is a second suggestion that can affect our tone. As we prepare to pray for or about public figures, we should remind ourselves that they are made in God's image. God highly esteems these people, however obvious their brokenness. God has made them in love and for love, however far they seem to have drifted from their moorings. They are persons: they are not simply the sum of their political opinions. They are subject to pressures, some of them enormous, from their constituencies, from their friends and enemies, and from whatever narrative about the good and successful life they have chosen to embrace. They are also persons who will one day be summoned before God to give an account of their leadership. Remembering these high truths will influence our praying. It will soften our hearts and deepen our appeals to God on their behalf.

Four suggestions regarding the content of public prayers
First, it can help to "pray off" a particular Bible text. There are a number of reasons for the wisdom of this. For one thing, the text will steer our own praying, filling in blind spots and guarding us from pursuing our own, or our church's, agenda. For another thing, it will help legitimize our prayer to those in our congregation who doubt that we see eye to eye with them politically

speaking. Actual prayers in the Bible, together with particular directions from the Bible on how to pray and behave publicly, can effectively guide our efforts: Nehemiah 1, Ephesians 1:15-23, Ephesians 3:14-21, Philippians 1:8-11, Colossians 1:9-10, 1 Peter 2:11-17, 1 Timothy 2:1-7, and any number of psalms come to mind.

Here is a second suggestion on content. We can include different types of prayers in our offerings. A helpful framework appears in the ACTS acrostic: Adoration, Confession, Thanksgiving, and Supplication. We have already alluded to confession. Think about adoration and thanksgiving. It generally won't do simply to pray for certain results (what we call prayers of supplication). That can be depressing, especially if the results elude us, which they often do. Our congregations need hope, and little engenders hope more effectively than prayers of thanks and praise. Such prayers remind us that God is in charge, that he is good, loving, and beautiful, and that he has shown us great public kindness in the past. Hope softens our discourse in church; it reminds us that, despite our frustration with the world and each other, all is fundamentally well and will one day be good beyond imagining.

A third suggestion regarding content is to pray "Trinitarian" prayers. Weaving the Father, the Son, and the Spirit into our public praying can help calm contentiousness by reminding our congregations of the riches that are at our disposal as we lay our concerns before God. Calling God "Father" reminds us that the one who oversees us and our broken world is kind. It reminds us further that he loves us enough to chasten us—which may help explain why some particularly troubling circumstances are persisting in our country despite our praying. Calling upon the "Son" reminds us that we have a human Brother who has tasted all our sorrows and temptations, and to whom we can, for that reason, bring every public reality that weighs upon us. It reminds us further that our Brother, despite appearances perhaps, rules over every person who represents us in government and over every social and economic trend that concerns us. Calling upon the "Son" reminds us, further, that we have a family member who will one day put everything right, establishing justice, truth, goodness, and beauty in every place and in every heart (including our own). Calling upon the Holy Spirit when we pray can calm our fear and anger by reminding us that help for a better world lies close at hand—not just in heaven and in some future that may seem a long way off—but deeply within us, to comfort, direct, and enable us as we seek to love our neighbors and one another as we should.

Here is a fourth suggestion on the content of our public prayers. Always keep in mind the distinction between moral principles and political strategies. This distinction will keep us from using prayer to endorse fallible strategies (say, to direct voting, or to endorse candidates, or to advocate for particular policies and laws). Remember that public praying, since it is completely controlled by the person who delivers it, can dress up coercion in holy clothing and, for that reason, can marginalize and infuriate people in the pews.

Prayer is the highest, and it can be the most powerful, thing we do. The highest things, if misused, can be the most harmful.

A sample of a public political prayer

I offered the following prayer publicly in August 2017 in response to the protest and counter-protest in Charlottesville, Virginia, over the proposed removal of a statue of Robert E. Lee from a public place. The violence of that day left many wounded and one person dead.

Let me read Psalm 130 before we pray together.

Out of the depths I cry to you, O LORD; O Lord, hear my voice. Let your ears be attentive to my cry for mercy. If you, O LORD, kept a record of sins, O Lord, who could stand? But with you there is forgiveness; therefore you are feared. I wait for the LORD, my soul waits, and in his word I put my hope. My soul waits for the Lord more than watchmen wait for the morning, more than watchmen wait for the morning. O Israel, put your hope in the LORD, for with the LORD is unfailing love and with him is full redemption. He himself will redeem Israel from all their sins.

Our Father, we cry to you from the depths. The events in Charlottesville trouble us profoundly. We grieve over the violence, the injury, and the senseless death in the streets there. We grieve that racism lingers so many years after the terrible war that ended slavery. We grieve that racism's public expression seems to be on the rise.

For many of us our grief is laced with anger and confusion. We see on TV the stony face of the young man who drove his car into a crowd of protestors and we are filled alternately with fury that he should do such a thing and perplexity over why he did it. There is a part of us that wants to hurt him as he hurt others. There is another part of us that wonders what it is about our life together as a nation that would foster and even sanction what he did.

We wonder, Lord, what we are supposed to do about Charlottesville, especially when we may be confused about the issue that led to the protests in the first place. Should we pull down every statue? Should we pull down any? If so, which ones—and why? Should we reflect more deeply on the events? If so, what should guide our reflections? Should we talk about our confusion and anger at church? If so, what should we say, and to whom?

Thank you for your voice speaking to us through the psalmist: *If you, O LORD, kept a record of sins, O Lord, who could stand?* We are confused, grieved, and justly angry. But we are also complicit. Each of us carries his own particular form of guilt. The bigotry we decry in others takes its own shape in us. We too stereotype people and diminish them: They may be young white men whose politics we fear and despise; they may be women who threaten our job security. We often treat people as obstructions to be blasted through, as enemies to be hurt, as nuisances to be avoided, and as resources to be exploited, but not as your image bearers, to be loved because we love you, even when we do not understand or like them.

Our sin runs deeper still. We treat people the way we do because we are afraid. We are like watchmen on the walls at night, peering into the darkness—but we have forgotten what we are searching for. We have forgotten that with you alone comes the morning. We have set our hopes elsewhere. Our aspirations have too often become our idols: a certain version of America, the implementation of a certain policy, job security, success, acceptance, pleasure, and freedom have too easily taken first place in our hearts. And because we cannot be sure of those things, we have rushed and manipulated and hurt to secure them.

Father, we are a reflection of our nation. In so many practical ways we have joined our country in forgetting you. Together with our neighbors we have lost our way. Together with them we have abandoned our first love and brought upon ourselves as a result the griefs of Charlottesville.

Forgive us, Father, by the cross of your Son. By your Spirit make that forgiveness, and the welcome that flows from it, so palpable and precious that we grow tired of setting our hopes in anyone or anything other than you. Order our politics more fully around your word, and less around our desires and preferences. Order our social hopes more fully around your steadfast love, and less around our fears and resentments. Teach us to fear you above all else.

Make your church beautiful—a place of love and honesty and humility and goodness so winsome and attractive that people throughout our beloved country are drawn to Jesus. Amen.

Some ideas for fruitful and peaceable small group discussion

The most effective way to build a culture of political peace in the church is to give church members actual experiences in which they discover that they can talk about politics without fighting. Here are some suggestions.

Holding a "Hot Topic" small group discussion

The aims of this discussion are two-fold: (1) to help participants distinguish more clearly between moral principles and political strategies; and (2) to help participants engage in a substantive political discussion that is not divisive.

1.) Pick a hot topic—say abortion, or tax policy, or creation care, or immigration, or same sex marriage.

   - Agree together that your aim in this session is not to change each other's minds, but rather to understand each other better.

   - Give each member in the group a specific amount of time to share his thinking about the issue—what troubles him about it and what he thinks should be done to address it. No interruptions or rejoinders permitted—only questions for clarification.

2.) Once everyone has spoken have a conversation together.

   - Seek to identify and distinguish between the moral principles and the political strategies that have surfaced in what has been said.

   - Try secondly to identify other principles and/or strategies that did not surface.

   - Try as well to identify if there are moral principles that are at odds with each other.

   - Throughout your time together listen very carefully to each other, trying particularly hard to understand the legitimate moral grounds for the strategies you disagree with.

3.) Don't end the meeting without praying together.

   - As you pray avoid "preaching prayers"— the sort of praying that seeks to assert your point of view.

   - Pray for the Lord to establish what is true and good and beautiful.

- Pray for wisdom regarding the issue and for the peace and testimony of the church as you wrestle over it with each other and with those outside the church.

Holding a "Fear and the Gospel" small group discussion

The aims of this discussion are three in number: (i) to remind participants that love and not fear should motivate and direct our public engagement and discourse; (ii) to disarm, or at least to reduce, political antagonism by encouraging participants to be vulnerable with each other about what they fear; and (iii) to increase participants' loving engagement with each other and with our politically polarized world by discovering together how the gospel can deliver them from their fears.

1.) Take 5 minutes to reflect privately on your worst case political and social scenario for America (socially, economically, sexually, in terms of public violence, whatever else comes to mind) and its impact on those you love. Then discuss that scenario with the group.

- What specifically are you afraid of losing, or of not having, in that scenario?

- Why are you afraid?

2.) Our political fears arise from our political idols—from making political figures and political solutions into God substitutes. Why is political idolatry a cause of fear? Answer with reference to Jeremiah's account of idolatry (from Jeremiah 2:11-13, below) and discuss the question that follows.

Has a nation ever changed its gods? (Yet they are not gods at all.) But my people have exchanged their Glory for worthless idols. Be appalled at this, O heavens, and shudder with great horror," declares the LORD. "My people have committed two sins: They have forsaken me, the spring of living water, and have dug their own cisterns, broken cisterns that cannot hold water.

- What idols do you detect in your "worst case scenario" fears?

3.) The gospel and our political fears. The following words of Paul are full of reference to hardship while also full of confident hope. Read them aloud together and then discuss the questions that follow.

*And we know that **in all things God works for the good** of those who love him, who have been called according to his purpose. For those God foreknew he also predestined to be **conformed to the likeness of his Son**, that he might be the firstborn among many brothers. And those he predestined, he also called; those he called, he also justified; those he justified, **he also glorified**. What, then, shall we say in response to this? If God is for us, who can be against us? **He who did not spare his own Son, but gave him up for us all-- how will he not also, along with him, graciously give us all things?** Who will bring any charge against those whom God has chosen? It is God who justifies. Who is he that condemns? Christ Jesus, who died-- more than that, who was raised to life-- is at the right hand of God and is also interceding for us. **Who shall separate us from the love of Christ?** Shall trouble or hardship or persecution or famine or nakedness or danger or sword? As it is written: "For your sake we face death all day long; we are considered as sheep to be slaughtered." No, in all these things we are more than conquerors through him who loved us. For I am convinced that neither death nor life, neither angels nor demons, neither the present nor the future, nor any powers, neither height nor depth, **nor anything else in all creation, will be able to separate us from the love of God that is in Christ Jesus our Lord**. (Romans 8:28-39)*

- What sorts of worst case scenarios does Paul envision as he writes, and how do they correspond to yours?

- Despite the enormous difficulties he faces, Paul is unafraid. How does the gospel address the uncertainties Paul was facing? Notice especially the phrases in bold.

- What might it look like for you to be politically active, but without fear? How might being safe in God's love influence your tone, or your form of activism, or anything else? In your answer, consider the worst case scenarios you discussed earlier.

4.) Pray together.

Begin thanking God for the promises and encouragements you noted in the bold segments of Romans 8. Then pray for one another and for our country.

Planning and holding a "hot topic" church forum together

The aim of this exercise is to help participants discover the best way to have a valuable church-wide political discussion—one that helps the church family love the world more effectively while at the same time maintaining and building the church family's love for one another. This exercise can be done by church leaders or a self-appointed group (in which case it would make sense to get your leadership's buy in on the plan). Once you have agreed on the topic to be discussed, plan your forum using the following guidelines.

1.) In your planning assume that at least two members of your planning group belong to different political parties (role play if necessary). This will help protect you from the sorts of blind spots that can lead to a public meeting that marginalizes and infuriates certain people.

2.) Your planning should take into consideration the following things:

- The three distinctions mentioned earlier in this chapter.

- An awareness of the role of idolatry (including your own) in political anger.

- The most effective format, timing, and setting for the forum: should it be a lecture, a panel with discussion, something else; should it happen during the Sunday school hour, on a week-day night, or some other time; should it be in the church facility, at someone's home, or at some other venue?

- Whom you want to invite: Is this something open to the public or is it in-house? Why?

- The most effective participants for the discussion: should the pastor(s) speak, should the elder(s), should outside speakers, should certain lay persons (if so, whom and why). This part of the planning should be particularly sensitive to the nuanced role of church power in political discussions—recalling the theocracy/influence and the principle/strategy distinctions made earlier in the chapter.

- The goals for the discussion: What do you want the people who attend to take away with them when they leave; what sort of church culture are you trying to build?).

3.) Don't rush the planning process—especially if this is a new initiative in your church.

4.) Pray a lot. Much is at stake in doing the forum wisely.

Having a cup of coffee with a Christian whose politics you despise

The aim of this exercise is to help participants get started in the sorts of important conversations we may not be familiar or comfortable with.

1.) Set up a get together with a friend, making clear as you do that you don't want to argue, but rather to listen and to understand that person's point of view.

2.) As you talk

- Determine that love (for your friend) and trust (in God) and not fear will drive your tone.

- Try to find common ground, beyond differing political strategies, in shared moral principles.

- Where you cannot agree, then agree to disagree.

- Try to plan on doing something together that advances the principles you agree on.

3.) Pray together at the end. Pray for the advancement of the moral principles that you agreed on. Pray for wisdom for each other, the church, and the country as we face the problems and opportunities that you talked about.

4.) Part as friends, and be sure as soon as possible to have the Lord's Supper together.

APPENDIX A

Below you will find the text of the Williamsburg Charter. Begun in the fall of 1986, it was revised over the course of two years in close consultation with a remarkably broad spectrum of political, academic, religious, and business leaders.[58] The framers presented it to the nation in Williamsburg, Virginia, on June 25, 1988 (the occasion of the two-hundredth anniversary of Virginia's call for the Bill of Rights), at which time the first one hundred nationally prominent figures signed it publicly (many others did so subsequently). The charter celebrates and reaffirms the meaning of religious freedom in our pluralistic day and has helped me immensely as I have wrestled with the issues addressed in this book.

The Williamsburg Charter: A National Celebration and Reaffirmation of the First Amendment Religious Liberty Clauses

Keenly aware of the high national purpose of commemorating the bicentennial of the United States Constitution, we who sign this Charter seek to celebrate the Constitution's greatness, and to call for a bold reaffirmation and reappraisal of its vision and guiding principles. In particular, we call for a fresh consideration of religious liberty in our time, and of the place of the First Amendment Religious Liberty clauses in our national life.

We gratefully acknowledge that the Constitution has been hailed as America's "chief export" and "the most wonderful work ever struck off at a given time by the brain and purpose of man." Today, two hundred years after its signing, the Constitution is not only the world's oldest, still-effective written constitution, but also the admired pattern of ordered liberty for countless people in many lands.

In spite of its enduring and universal qualities, however, some provisions of the Constitution are now the subject of widespread controversy in the United States. One area of intense controversy concerns the First Amendment Religious

Liberty clauses, whose mutually reinforcing provisions act as a double guarantee of religious liberty, one part barring the making of any law "respecting an establishment of religion" and the other barring any law "prohibiting the free exercise thereof."

The First Amendment Religious Liberty provisions epitomize the Constitution's visionary realism. They were, as James Madison said, the "true remedy" to the predicament of religious conflict they originally addressed, and they well express the responsibilities and limits of the state with respect to liberty and justice.

Our commemoration of the Constitution's bicentennial must therefore go beyond celebration to rededication. Unless this is done, an irreplaceable part of national life will be endangered, and a remarkable opportunity for the expansion of liberty will be lost.

For we judge that the present controversies over religion in public life pose both a danger and an opportunity. There is evident danger in the fact that certain forms of politically reassertive religion in parts of the world are, in principle, enemies of democratic freedom and a source of deep social antagonism. There is also evident opportunity in the growing philosophical and cultural awareness that all people live by commitments and ideals, that value-neutrality is impossible in the ordering of society, and that we are on the edge of a promising moment for a fresh assessment of pluralism and liberty. It is with an eye to both the promise and the peril that we publish this Charter and pledge ourselves to its principles.

We readily acknowledge our continuing differences. Signing this Charter implies no pretense that we believe the same things or that our differences over policy proposals, legal interpretations and philosophical groundings do not ultimately matter. The truth is not even that what unites us is deeper than what divides us, for differences over belief are the deepest and least easily negotiated of all.

The Charter sets forth a renewed national compact, in the sense of a solemn mutual agreement between parties, on how we view the place of religion in American life and how we should contend with each other's deepest differences in the public sphere. It is a call to a vision of public life that will allow conflict to lead to consensus, religious commitment to reinforce political civility. In this way, diversity is not a point of weakness but a source of strength.

I. A TIME FOR REAFFIRMATION

We believe, in the first place, that the nature of the Religious Liberty clauses must be understood before the problems surrounding them can be resolved. We therefore affirm both their cardinal assumptions and the reasons for their crucial national importance.

With regard to the assumptions of the First Amendment Religious Liberty clauses, we hold three to be chief:

1. The Inalienable Right

Nothing is more characteristic of humankind than the natural and inescapable drive toward meaning and belonging, toward making sense of life and finding community in the world. As fundamental and precious as life itself, this "will to meaning" finds expression in ultimate beliefs, whether theistic or nontheistic, transcendent or naturalistic, and these beliefs are most our own when a matter of conviction rather than coercion. They are most our own when, in the words of George Mason, the principal author of the Virginia Declaration of Rights, they are "directed only by reason and conviction, not by force or violence."

As James Madison expressed it in his Memorial and Remonstrance, "The Religion then of every man must be left to the conviction and conscience of every man; and it is the right of every man to exercise it as these may dictate. This right is in its nature an unalienable right."

Two hundred years later, despite dramatic changes in life and a marked increase of naturalistic philosophies in some parts of the world and in certain sectors of our society, this right to religious liberty based upon freedom of conscience remains fundamental and inalienable. While particular beliefs may be true or false, better or worse, the right to reach, hold, exercise them freely, or change them, is basic and nonnegotiable.

Religious liberty finally depends on neither the favors of the state and its officials nor the vagaries of tyrants or majorities. Religious liberty in a democracy is a right that may not be submitted to vote and depends on the outcome of no election. A society is only as just and free as it is respectful of this right, especially toward the beliefs of its smallest minorities and least popular communities.

The right to freedom of conscience is premised not upon science, nor upon social utility, not upon pride of species. Rather, it is premised upon the inviolable dignity of the human person. It is the foundation of, and is integrally related to, all other rights and freedoms secured by the Constitution. This basic civil liberty is clearly acknowledged in the Declaration of Independence and is ineradicable from the long tradition of rights and liberties from which the Revolution sprang.

2. The Ever Present Danger

No threat to freedom of conscience and religious liberty has historically been greater than the coercions of both Church and State. These two institutions—the one religious, the other political—have through the centuries succumbed to the temptation of coercion in their claims over minds and souls. When these institutions and their claims have been combined, it has too often resulted in terrible violations of human liberty and dignity. They are so combined when the sword and purse of the State are in the hands of the Church, or when the State usurps the mantle of the Church so as to coerce the conscience and compel belief. These and other such confusions of religion and state authority represent the misordering of religion and government which it is the purpose of the Religious Liberty provisions to prevent.

Authorities and orthodoxies have changed, kingdoms and empires have come and gone, yet as John Milton once warned, "new Presbyter is but old priest write large." Similarly, the modern persecutor of religion is but ancient tyrant with more refined instruments of control. Moreover, many of the greatest crimes against conscience of this century have been committed, not by religious authorities, but by ideologues virulently opposed to traditional religion.

Yet whether ancient or modern, issuing from religion or ideology, the result is the same: religious and ideological orthodoxies, when politically established, lead only too naturally toward what Roger Williams calls a "spiritual rape" that coerces the conscience and produces "rivers of civil blood" that stain the record of human history.

Less dramatic but also lethal to freedom, and the chief menace to religious liberty today, is the expanding power of government control over personal behavior and the institutions of society, when the government acts not so much in deliberate hostility to, but in reckless disregard of, communal belief and personal conscience.

Thanks principally to the wisdom of the First Amendment, the American experience is different. But even in America where state-established orthodoxies are unlawful and the state is constitutionally limited, religious liberty can never be taken for granted. It is a rare achievement that requires constant protection.

3. The Most Nearly Perfect Solution

Knowing well that "nothing human can be perfect" (James Madison) and that the Constitution was not "a faultless work" (Gouverneur Morris), the Framers nevertheless saw the First Amendment as a "true remedy" and the most nearly perfect solution yet devised for properly ordering the relationship of religion and the state in a free society.

There have been occasions when the protections of the First Amendment have been overridden or imperfectly applied. Nonetheless, the First Amendment is a momentous decision for religious liberty, the most important political decision for religious liberty and public justice in the history of humankind. Limitation upon religious liberty is allowable only where the State has borne a heavy burden of proof that the limitation is justified—not by any ordinary public interest, but by a supreme public necessity—and that no less restrictive alternative to limitation exists.

The Religious Liberty clauses are a brilliant construct in which both No establishment and Free exercise serve the ends of religious liberty and freedom of conscience. No longer can sword, purse, and sacred mantle be equated. Now, the government is barred from using religion's mantle to become a confessional State, and from allowing religion to use the government's sword and purse to become a coercing Church. In this new order, the freedom of the government from religious control and the freedom of religion from government control are a double guarantee of the protection of rights. No faith is referred or prohibited; for where there is no state-definable orthodoxy, there can be no state-punishable heresy.

With regard to the reasons why the First Amendment Religious Liberty clauses are important for the nation today, we hold five to be preeminent:

1. The First Amendment Religious Liberty provisions have both a logical and historical priority in the Bill of Rights. They have logical priority because the security of all rights rests upon the recognition that they are neither given by the state, nor can they be taken away by the state. Such rights are inherent in the inviolability of the human person. History demonstrates that unless these rights are protected our society's slow, painful progress toward freedom would not have been possible.

2. The First Amendment Religious Liberty provisions lie close to the distinctiveness of the American experiment. The uniqueness of the American way of disestablishment and its consequences have often been more obvious to foreign observers such as Alexis de Tocqueville and Lord James Bryce, who wrote that "Of all the differences between the Old world and the New, this is perhaps the most salient." In particular, the Religious Liberty clauses are vital to harnessing otherwise centrifugal forces such as personal liberty and social diversity, thus sustaining republican vitality while making possible a necessary measure of national concord.

3. The First Amendment Religious Liberty provisions are the democratic world's most salient alternative to the totalitarian repression of human rights and provide a corrective to unbridled nationalism and religious warfare around the world.

4. The First Amendment Religious Liberty provisions provide the United States' most distinctive answer to one of the world's most pressing questions in the late-twentieth century. They address the problem: How do we live with each other's deepest

differences? How do religious convictions and political freedom complement rather than threaten each other on a small planet in a pluralistic age? In a world in which bigotry, fanaticism, terrorism and the state control of religion are all too common responses to these questions, sustaining the justice and liberty of the American arrangement is an urgent moral task.

5. The First Amendment Religious Liberty provisions give American society a unique position in relation to both the First and Third worlds. Highly modernized like the rest of the First World, yet not so secularized, this society—largely because of religious freedom—remains, like most of the Third World, deeply religious. This fact, which is critical for possibilities of better human understanding, has not been sufficiently appreciated in American self-understanding, or drawn upon in American diplomacy and communication throughout the world.

In sum, as much if not more than any other single provision in the entire Constitution, the Religious Liberty provisions hold the key to American distinctiveness and American destiny. Far from being settled by the interpretations of judges and historians, the last word on the First Amendment likely rests in a chapter yet to be written, documenting the unfolding drama of America. If religious liberty is neglected, all civil liberties will suffer. If it is guarded and sustained, the American experiment will be the more secure.

II. A TIME FOR REAPPRAISAL

Much of the current controversy about religion and politics neither reflects the highest wisdom of the First Amendment nor serves the best interests of the disputants or the nations. We therefore call for a critical reappraisal of the course and consequences of such controversy. Four widespread errors have exacerbated the controversy needlessly.

1. The Issue Is Not Only What We Debate, but How

The debate about religion in public life is too often misconstrued as a clash of ideologies alone, pitting "secularists" against the "sectarians" or vice versa. Though competing and even contrary worldviews are involved, the controversy is not solely ideological. It also flows from a breakdown in understanding of how personal and communal beliefs should be related to public life.

The American republic depends upon the answers to two questions. By what ultimate truths ought we to live? And how should these be related to public life? The first question is personal, but has a public dimension because of the connection between beliefs and public virtue. The American answer to the first question is that the government is excluded from giving an answer. The second question, however, is thoroughly public in character, and a public answer is appropriate and necessary to the well-being of this society.

This second question was central to the idea of the First Amendment. The Religious Liberty provisions are not "articles of faith" concerned with the substance of particular doctrines or of policy issues. They are "articles of peace" concerned with the constitutional constraints and the shared prior understanding within which the American people can engage their differences in a civil manner and thus provide for both religious liberty and stable public government.

Conflicts over the relationship between deeply held beliefs and public policy will remain a continuing feature of democratic life. They do not discredit the First Amendment, but confirm its wisdom and point to the need to distinguish the Religious Liberty clauses from the particular controversies they address. The clauses can never be divorced form the controversies they address, but should always be held distinct. In the public discussion, an open commitment to the constraints and standards of the clauses should precede and accompany debate over the controversies.

2. The Issue Is Not Sectarian, but National

The role of religion in American public life is too often devalued or dismissed in public debate, as though the American people's historically vital religious traditions were at best a purely private matter and at worst essentially sectarian and divisive.

Such a position betrays a failure of civil respect for the convictions of others. It also underestimates the degree to which the Framers relied on the American people's religious convictions to be what Tocqueville described as "the first of their political institutions." In America, this crucial public role has been played by diverse beliefs, not so much despite disestablishment as because of disestablishment.

The Founders knew well that the republic they established represented an audacious gamble against long historical odds. This form of government depends upon ultimate beliefs, for otherwise we have no right to the rights by which it thrives, yet rejects any official formulation of them. The republic will therefore always remain an "undecided experiment" that stands or falls by the dynamism of its nonestablished faiths.

3. The Issue Is Larger Than the Disputants

Recent controversies over religion and public life have too often become a form of warfare in which individuals, motives and reputations have been impugned. The intensity of the debate is commensurate with the importance of the issues debated, but to those engaged in this warfare we present two arguments for reappraisal and restraint.

The lesser argument is one of expediency and is based on the ironic fact that each side has become the best argument for the other. One side's excesses have become the other side's arguments; one side's extremists the other side's recruiters. The danger is that, as the ideological warfare becomes self-perpetuating, more serious issues and broader national interests will be forgotten and the bitterness deepened.

The more important argument is one of principle and is based on the fact that the several sides have pursued their objectives in ways which contradict their own best ideals. Too often, for example, religious believers have been uncharitable, liberals have been illiberal, conservatives have been insensitive to tradition, champions of tolerance have been intolerant, defenders of free speech have been censorious, and citizens of a republic based on democratic accommodations have succumbed to a habit of relentless confrontation.

4. The Issue Is Understandably Threatening

The First Amendment's meaning is too often debated in ways that ignore the genuine grievances or justifiable fears of opposing points of view. This happens when the logic of opposing arguments favors either an unwarranted intrusion of religion into public life or an unwarranted exclusion of religion from it. History plainly shows that with religious control over government, political freedom dies; with political control over religion, religious freedom dies.

The First Amendment has contributed to avoiding both these perils, but this happy experience is no cause for complacency. Though the United States has escaped the worst excesses experienced elsewhere in the world, the republic has shown two distinct tendencies of its own, one in the past and one today.

In earliest times, though lasting well into the twentieth century, there was a de facto semi-establishment of one religion in the United States: a generalized Protestantism given dominant status in national institutions, especially in the public schools. This development was largely approved by Protestants, but widely opposed by non-Protestants, including Catholics and Jews.

In more recent times, and partly in reaction, constitutional jurisprudence has tended, in the view of many, to move toward the de facto semi-establishment of a wholly secular understanding of the origin, nature and destiny of humankind and of the American nation. During this period, the exclusion of teaching about the role of religion in society, based partly upon a misunderstanding of First Amendment decisions, has ironically resulted in giving a dominant status to such wholly secular understandings in many national institutions. Many secularists appear as unconcerned over the consequences of this development as were Protestants unconcerned about their de facto establishment earlier.

Such de facto establishments, though seldom extreme, usually benign and often unwitting, are the source of grievances and fears among the several parties in current controversies. Together with the encroachments of the expanding modern state, such de facto establishments, as much as any official establishment, are likely to remain a threat to freedom and justice for all.

Justifiable fears are raised by those who advocate theocracy or the coercive power of law to establish a "Christian American." While this advocacy is and should be legally protected, such proposals contradict freedom of conscience and the genius of the Religious Liberty provisions.

At the same time there are others who raise justifiable fears of an unwarranted exclusion of religion from public life. The assertion of moral judgments as though they were morally neutral, and interpretations of the "wall of separation" that would exclude religious expression and argument from public life, also contradict freedom of conscience and the genius of the provisions.

Civility obliges citizens in a pluralistic society to take great care in using words and casting issues. The communications media have a primary role, and thus a special responsibility, in shaping public opinion and debate. Words such as *public, secular,* and *religious* should be free from discriminatory bias. "Secular purpose," for example, should not mean "nonreligious purpose" but "general public purpose." Otherwise, the impression is gained that "public is equivalent to secular; religion is equivalent to private." Such equations are neither accurate nor just. Similarly, it is false to equate "public" and "governmental." In a society that sets store by the necessary limits on government, there are many spheres of life that are public but nongovernmental.

Two important conclusions follow from a reappraisal of the present controversies over religion in public life. First, the process of adjustment and readjustment to the constraints and standards of the Religious Liberty provisions is an ongoing requirement of American democracy. The Constitution is not a self-interpreting, self-executing document; and the prescriptions of the Religious Liberty provisions cannot by themselves resolve the myriad confusions and ambiguities surrounding the right ordering of the relationship between religion and government in a free society. The Framers clearly understood that the Religious Liberty provisions provide the legal construct for what must be an ongoing process of adjustment and mutual give-and-take in a democracy.

We are keenly aware that, especially over state-supported education, we as a people must continue to wrestle with the complex connections between religion and the transmission of moral values in a pluralistic society. Thus, we cannot have, and should not seek, a definitive, once for all solution to the questions that will continue to surround the Religious Liberty provisions.

Second, the need for such a readjustment today can best be addressed by remembering that the two clauses are essentially one provision for preserving religious liberty. Both parts, No Establishment and Free Exercise, are to be comprehensively understood as being in the service of religious liberty as a positive good. At the heart of the Establishment clause is the prohibition of state sponsorship of religion and at the heart of Free Exercise clause is the prohibition of state interference with religious liberty.

No sponsorship means that the State must leave to the free citizenry the public expression of ultimate beliefs, religious or otherwise, providing only that no expression is excluded from, and none governmentally favored, in the continuing democratic discourse.

No interference means the assurance of voluntary religious expression free from governmental intervention. This includes placing religious expression on an equal footing with all other forms of expression in genuinely public forums.

No sponsorship and no interference together mean fair opportunity. That is to say, all faiths are free to enter vigorously into public life and to exercise such influence as their followers and ideas engender. Such democratic exercise of influence as is in the best tradition of American voluntarism and is not an unwarranted "imposition" or "establishment."

III. A TIME FOR RECONSTITUTION

We believe, finally, that the time is ripe for a genuine expansion of democratic liberty, and that this goal may be attained through a new engagement of citizens in a debate that is reordered in accord with constitutional first principles and considerations of the common good. This amounts to no less than the reconstitution of a free republican people in our day. Careful consideration of three precepts would advance this possibility:

1. The Criteria Must Be Multiple

Reconstitution requires the recognition that the great dangers in interpreting the Constitution today are either to release interpretation from any demanding criteria or to narrow the criteria excessively. The first relaxes the necessary restraining force of the Constitution, while the second overlooks the insights that have arisen from the Constitution in two centuries of national experience.

Religious liberty is the only freedom in the First Amendment to be given two provisions. Together the clauses form a strong bulwark against suppression of religious liberty, yet they emerge from a series of dynamic tensions which cannot ultimately be relaxed. The Religious Liberty provisions grow out of an understanding not only of rights and a due recognition of faiths but of realism and a due recognition of factions. They themselves reflect both faith and skepticism. They raise questions of equality and liberty, majority rule and minority rights, individual convictions and communal tradition.

The Religious Liberty provisions must be understood both in terms of the Framers' intentions and history's sometimes surprising results. Interpreting and applying them today requires not only historical research but moral and political reflection.

The intention of the Framers is therefore a necessary but insufficient criterion for interpreting and applying the Constitution. But applied by itself, without any consideration of immutable principles of justice, the intention can easily be wielded as a weapon for governmental or sectarian causes, some quoting Jefferson and brandishing No Establishment and others citing Madison and brandishing Free Exercise. Rather, we must take the purpose and text of the Constitution seriously, sustain the principles behind the words and add an appreciation of the many-sided genius of the First Amendment and its complex development over time.

2. The Consensus Must Be Dynamic

Reconstitution requires a shared understanding of the relationship between the Constitution and the society it is to serve. The Framers understood that the Constitution is more than parchment and ink. The principles embodied in the document must be affirmed in practice by a free people since these principles reflect everything that constitutes the essential forms and substance of their society—the institutions, customs and ideals as well as the laws. Civic vitality and the effectiveness of law can be undermined when they overlook this broader cultural context of the Constitution.

Notable, in this connection is the striking absence today of any national consensus about religious liberty as a positive good. Yet religious liberty is indisputably what the Framers intended and what the First Amendment has preserved. Far from being a matter of exemption, exception or even toleration, religious liberty is an unalienable right. Far from being a subcategory of free speech or a constitutional redundancy, religious liberty is distinct and foundational. Far from being simply an individual right religious liberty is a positive social good. Far from denigrating religion as a social or political "problem," the separation of Church and State is both the saving of religion from the temptation of political power and an achievement inspired in large part by religion itself. Far from weakening religion, disestablishment has, as an historical fact, enabled it to flourish.

In light of the First Amendment, government should stand in relation to the churches, synagogues and other communities of faith as the guarantor of freedom. In light of the First Amendment, the churches, synagogues and other communities of faith stand in relation to the government as generators of faith, and therefore contribute to the spiritual and moral foundations of democracy. Thus, the government acts as a safeguard, but not the source, of freedom for faiths, whereas the churches and synagogues act as a source, but not the safeguard, of faiths for freedom.

The Religious Liberty provisions work for each other and for the federal idea as a whole. Neither established nor excluded, neither preferred nor proscribed, each faith (whether transcendent or naturalistic) is brought into a relationship with the government so that each is separated from the state in terms of its institutions, but democratically related to the state in terms of individuals and its ideas.

The result is neither a naked public square where all religion is excluded, nor a sacred public square with any religion established or semi-established.

The result, rather, is a civil public square in which citizens of all religious faiths, or none, engage one another in the continuing democratic discourse.

3. The Compact Must Be Mutual

Reconstitution of a free republican people requires the recognition that religious liberty is a universal right joined to a universal duty to respect that right.

In turns and twists of history, victims of religious discrimination have often later become perpetrators. In the famous image of Roger Williams, those at the helm of the Ship of State forget they were once under the hatches. They have, he said, "One weight for themselves when they are under the hatches, and another for others when they come to the helm." They show themselves, said James Madison, "as ready to set up an establishment which is to take them in as they were to pull down that which shut them out." Thus, benignly or otherwise, Protestants have treated Catholics as they were once treated, and secularists have done likewise with both.

Such inconsistencies are the natural seedbed for the growth of a de facto establishment. Against such inconsistencies we affirm that a right for one is a right for another and a responsibility for all. A right for a Protestant is a right for an Orthodox is a right for a Catholic is a right for a Jew is a right for a Humanist is a right for a Mormon is a right for a Muslim is a right for a Buddhist—and for the followers of any other faith within the wide bounds of the republic.

That rights are universal and responsibilities mutual is both the premise and the promise of democratic pluralism. The First Amendment, in this sense, is the epitome of public justice and serves as the golden rule for civic life. Rights are best guarded and responsibilities best exercised when each person and group guards for all others the rights they wish guarded for themselves. Whereas the wearer of the English crown is officially the Defender of the Faith, all who uphold the American Constitution are defenders of the rights of all faiths.

From this axiom, that rights are universal and responsibilities mutual, derive guidelines for conducting public debates involving religion in a manner that is democratic and civil. These guidelines are not, and must not be, mandated by law. But they are, we believe, necessary to reconstitute and revitalize the American understanding of the role of religion in a free society.

First, those who claim the right to dissent should assume the responsibility to debate: Commitment to democratic pluralism assumes the coexistence within one political community of groups whose ultimate faith commitments may be incompatible, yet whose common commitment to social unity and diversity does justice to both the requirements of individual conscience and the wider community. A general consent to the obligations of citizenship is therefore inherent in the American experiment, both as a founding principle ("We the people") and as a matter of daily practice.

There must always be room for those who do not wish to participate in the public ordering of our common life, who desire to pursue their own religious witness separately as conscience dictates. But at the same time, for those who do wish to participate, it should be understood that those claiming the right to dissent should assume the responsibility to debate. As this responsibility is exercised, the characteristic American formula of individual liberty complemented by respect for the opinions of others permits differences to be asserted, yet a broad, active community of understanding to be sustained.

Second, those who claim the right to criticize should assume the responsibility to comprehend: One of the ironies of democratic life is that freedom of conscience is jeopardized by false tolerance as well as by outright intolerance. Genuine tolerance considers contrary views fairly and judges them on merit. Debased tolerance so refrains from making any judgment that it refuses to listen at all. Genuine tolerance honestly weighs honest differences and promotes both impartiality and pluralism. Debased tolerance results in indifference to the differences that vitalize a pluralistic democracy.

Central to the difference between genuine and debased tolerance is the recognition that peace and truth must be held in tension. Pluralism must not be confused with, and is in fact endangered by, philosophical and ethical indifference. Commitment to strong, clear philosophical and ethical ideas need not imply either intolerance or opposition to democratic pluralism. On the contrary, democratic pluralism requires an agreement to be locked in public argument over disagreements of consequence within the bonds of civility.

The right to argue for any public policy is a fundamental right for every citizen; respecting that right is a fundamental responsibility for all other citizens.

When any view is expressed, all must uphold as constitutionally protected its advocate's right to express it. But others are free to challenge that view as politically pernicious, philosophically false, ethically evil, theologically idolatrous, or simply absurd, as the case may be seen to be.

Unless this tension between peace and truth is respected, civility cannot be sustained. In that event, tolerance degenerates into either apathetic relativism or a dogmatism as uncritical of itself as it is uncomprehending of others. The result is a general corruption of principled public debate.

Third, those who claim the right to influence should accept the responsibility not to inflame: Too often in recent disputes over religion and public affairs, some have insisted that any evidence of religious influence on public policy represents an establishment of religion and is therefore precluded as an improper "imposition." Such exclusion of religion from public life is historically unwarranted, philosophically inconsistent and profoundly undemocratic. The Framers' intention is indisputably ignored when public policy debates can appeal to the theses of Adam Smith and Karl Marx, or Charles Darwin and Sigmund Freud but not to the Western religious tradition in general and the Hebrew and Christian Scriptures in particular. Many of the most dynamic social movements in American history, including that of civil rights, were legitimately inspired and shaped by religious motivation.

Freedom of conscience and the right to influence public policy on the basis of religiously informed ideas are inseverably linked. In short, a key to democratic renewal is the fullest possible participation in the most open possible debate.

Religious liberty and democratic civility are also threatened, however, from another quarter. Overreacting to an improper veto on religion in public life, many have used religious language and images not for the legitimate influencing of policies but to inflame politics. Politics is indeed an extension of ethics and therefore engages religious principles; but some err by refusing to recognize that there is a distinction, though not a separation, between religion and politics. As a result, they bring to politics a misplaced absoluteness that idolizes politics, "Satanizes" their enemies and politicizes their own faith.

Even the most morally informed policy positions involve prudential judgments as well as pure principle. Therefore, to make an absolute equation of principles and policies inflates politics and does violence to reason, civil life and faith itself. Politics has recently been inflamed by a number of confusions: the confusion of personal religious affiliation with qualification or disqualifications for public office; the confusion of claims to divine guidance with claims to divine endorsement; the confusion of government neutrality among faiths with government indifference or hostility to religion.

Fourth, those who claim the right to participate should accept the responsibility to persuade: Central to the American experience is the power of political persuasion. Growing partly from principle and partly from the pressures of democratic pluralism, commitment to persuasion is the corollary of the belief that the conscience is inviolable, coercion of conscience is evil, and the public interest is best served by consent hard won from vigorous debate. Those who believe themselves privy to the will of history brook no argument and need never tarry for consent. But to those who subscribe to the idea of government by the consent of the governed, compelled beliefs are a violation of the first principles. The natural logic of the Religious Liberty provisions is to foster a political culture of persuasion which admits the challenge of opinions from all sources.

Arguments for public policy should be more than private convictions shouted out loud. For persuasion to be principled, private convictions should be translated into publicly accessible claims. Such public claims should be made publicly accessible for two reasons: first, because they must engage those who do not share the same private convictions, and second, because they should be directed toward the common good.

RENEWAL OF THE FIRST PRINCIPLES

We who live in the third century of the American republic can learn well from the past as we look to the future. Our Founders were both idealists and realists. Their confidence in human abilities was tempered by their skepticism about human nature. Aware of what was new in their times, they also knew the need for renewal in times after theirs. " No free government, or the blessings of liberty," wrote George Mason in 1776, "can be preserved to any people, but by a firm adherence to justice, moderation, temperance, frugality, and virtue, and by frequent recurrence to fundamental principles."

True to the ideals and realism of that vision, we who sign this Charter, people of many and various beliefs, pledge ourselves to the enduring precepts of the First Amendment as the cornerstone of the American experiment in liberty under law.

We address ourselves to our fellow citizens, daring to hope that the strongest desire of the greatest number is for the common good. We are firmly persuaded that the principles asserted here require a fresh consideration, and that the renewal of religious liberty is crucial to sustain a free people that would remain free. We therefore commit ourselves to speak, write and act according to this vision and these principles. We urge our fellow citizens to do the same.

To agree on such guiding principles and to achieve such a compact will not be easy. Whereas a law is a command directed to us, a compact is a promise that must proceed freely from us. To achieve it demands a measure of the vision, sacrifice and perseverance shown by our Founders. Their task was to defy the past, seeing and securing religious liberty against the terrible precedents of history. Ours is to challenge the future, sustaining vigilance and broadening protections against every new menace, including that of our own complacency. Knowing the unquenchable desire for freedom, they lit a beacon. It is for us who know its blessings to keep it burning brightly.

APPENDIX B

What follows is the text of an in-house document, developed by the Three Village Church, E. Setauket, New York, offered here as an incentive to churches to develop similar documents.

Christian Citizenship: Some Principles and Practices

Christians possess dual citizenship. They belong to the kingdom of God and they also belong to particular nations. In recent years much discussion (heated at times) has centered on how in practical terms we are to live out this dual citizenship. This pamphlet contains a series of 11 principles that the leadership of Three Village Church believes should govern our approach to these matters.

1. God is Creator and Lord of all things, and has called us to subdue all things to His glory (Gen. 1:1; Rev. 4:11; Gen. 1:28; Rom. 11:36; 1 Cor. 10:31).

   We therefore affirm that every sphere of life (including the political) is important and spiritual. For this reason we will seek to be informed of the political and social issues in our country and world.

2. God's Word is given to equip the Christian for every good work (2 Tim. 3:16).

   We therefore affirm that there is no issue in public life to which the Bible does not speak in some way. We further affirm that there is no single issue in public life that should alone occupy the attention of every Christian.

3. God has commissioned Christians to be "salt and light" (Matt. 5:13; Mark 9:50; Matt. 5:14; Matt. 5:16).

   Each of us will therefore act upon his or her convictions in the social and political realms of life, employing all lawful means available.

Furthermore, we will be sensitive to how we act, remembering that how we present ourselves is at least as important as the substance of our convictions.

4.   The governments of this world are established by God as necessary evils to limit the potential reign of evil (Rom. 13:1–7).

We will therefore work within the law, respecting it for God's sake, rather than because it is sound in every way. We will also respect those who represent the law (police, magistrates, elected officials). There may be extreme instances so troublesome to the conscience that some of us may choose to disobey the law for Christ's sake. But we will do so humbly and be prepared to endure the consequences of our decision.

5.   Jesus taught us to make a distinction between the kingdom of God and the kingdoms of this world, reminding us that we have responsibilities to both (Mark 12:17). (The first, to which our deepest allegiance belongs, is international and spiritual, crossing all the barriers set by the second. It is enforced by the working of the Holy Spirit upon the heart through the Word of God in response to prayer.)

We will therefore resist the temptation to equate the United States, or any human institution, or any human leader (past, present, or future— whether a nation or a political party or a government program) with God's kingdom.

We will also, therefore, limit our expectations regarding societal change through political means, remembering that the key to all such change is not a particular set of laws, or a party, or a government, but the working of the gospel in the hearts of people, one by one.

We will also, therefore, commit ourselves to prayer as the primary most powerful means of bringing change to society. We will pray, in particular, that rulers will maintain both social order and religious freedom of expression, since these are both necessary for the Word of God to be lived out and proclaimed (1 Tim. 2:1–7).

6. The church of Jesus Christ, representing the present and coming reign of Jesus Christ, has been given a priority mandate to proclaim the gospel (1 Pet. 2:9; Matt. 28:19–20).

    Therefore, we will take care not to allow our involvement in political and social issues to either divert us from this task or divide us unnecessarily from each other or from those whom we are seeking to reach.

7. A distinction must be made in Christian thinking between the role of the individual Christian and the role of the "church-as-the-church" in addressing issues of Christian citizenship. The individual is free (and obligated) to be involved in lobbying, voting, marching, etc. according to his conscience. The church-as-the-church, on the other hand, must preserve her primary task.

    Therefore, our church will encourage people to be informed and active citizens, but will take care not to permit our corporate involvement in social and political issues to divert our attention unduly from fulfilling the Great Commission.

8. A distinction must be made in Christian thinking between principles and strategies. Principles are expression of moral law, and it is the duty of individuals and of the church-as-the-church to promote and uphold God's law. Strategies are the flawed and varied efforts we engage in to implement the moral law in society. In the realm of strategies the church-as-the-church must ordinarily give individual Christians the freedom and responsibility to discuss and act according to their own best judgment.

    Therefore, we will be careful not to prescribe strategies, nor to give the impression that we are doing so.

9. Christians are ambassadors for Christ, exiles on earth, representing in public life their true King and homeland (2 Cor. 5:20; 1 Pet. 2:11–17).

    We will therefore seek to live exemplary public lives so as to give honor to our true Sovereign. We will never be content to limit our civic and social behavior by the questions, "Is it legal?" or "Can I get away with it?" We will always ask further questions, such as, "Is what I am doing moral?" and, "Does this please Christ?" and, "Will what I am about to do dishonor or inhibit Christ's place in the public mind?"

10. The Christian citizen is properly motivated by the desire to be faithful to God and not the need to see his social/political agenda (however worthy) succeed (Ps. 46:10; 1 Sam. 24:1–3).

   Therefore, we will patiently pursue what we deem right, even if the "right" never materializes. Furthermore, we will resist the tendency, born of impatience, to employ unworthy means to realize our dreams more quickly.

11. The gospel champions the dignity of the individual and the freedom of the conscience (Gen. 1:26–27; Rom. 14:23; 2 Cor. 5:11; 2 Cor. 9:7; 1 Tim. 2:1–2).

   Therefore, we will continually ask, "How will my civic actions affect in the long run the freedom of all religious faith and practice in my country?" We will bear in mind that mixing politics and religion too tightly can violently polarize a nation and lead to the loss of religious freedom.

APPENDIX C

A Vision of Incarnation

What follows is a portion of the vision statement of Emmanuel Presbyterian Church, begun in 2000 next to Columbia University on the Upper West Side of Manhattan. Values 3 through 5 in particular seek to give expression to the notion that the believer's public responsibility and influence are much broader than his political activism as it is defined in our times.

Our Core Values: What Are We Passionate About?

1. **Vitality through knowing Jesus Christ**: We seek much more than Christian information: we seek to see and know Jesus as he reveals God to us in the gospel, for to see him is to experience continual renewal in our lives and ministries. We know Jesus better through regular and intentional participation in the means of grace—fellowship, Bible study, prayer, the sacraments, and a missional life. Worship, public and private, is very important to us.

2. **Community life**: We strongly believe that significant growth happens only in the context of safe, honest, and caring friendships. For this reason we provide small group and one-on-one mentoring relationships.

3. **Holistic ministry**: We look to see the influence of Jesus' transforming lordship in all things and in the whole of our lives. Teaching the Bible and showing love in practical ways are of equal importance—as are evangelism and academics, prayer and social justice, doctrinal orthodoxy and beautiful music, strong relationships and responsible care for the environment. How we think at and about work and school is as important as how we think at and about church.

4. **Incarnational living:** We seek to emulate Jesus' *modus operandi* in our pattern of life and ministry: Jesus, lovingly committed to our

healing, fully entered our experience while remaining faithful to his Father. Even so, we seek, lovingly committed to our world's healing, to enter genuinely and faithfully into the communities and workplaces where God has placed us, while also seeking to be faithful to Christ in those places. Such engagement meant suffering for Jesus, and we should not be surprised or disheartened if it means suffering for us.

5. **City-loving attitude**: We choose to love New York City—its people and its institutions. We choose neither to stand aloof from the city nor to be swallowed up by its values where they are fallen. Instead we choose to be its friends—to feel its pains, to enjoy its glories, to pray for its peace, and to subvert it to the King by sacrificial love. We exist not to make ourselves a great church but to make New York a great city.

6. **Local focus**: We see ourselves as a local church, existing to enhance Jesus' loving reign in our part of town, especially at the university and among the local poor. We are not just *in* this part of town, nor are we all *from* here; but we are *for* this area. Over time we would rejoice to know that the neighborhood in and around Morningside Heights, including West Harlem, Harlem Heights, and Manhattan Valley, is a better place—a kinder place, a more just place—more reflective of God's plan, because we have been here.

7. **Church planting**: We believe that church planting is our Lord's preferred means of seeing his kingdom expand. We ourselves are a church plant and we seek to plant other urban churches, especially in New York.

8. **Prayer for the victory and honor of God over all things and all people**: We believe that God is at work through the gospel to overthrow the deeply imbedded antipathy towards him that exists in every person, every activity, and every institution in this world—including the church. We further believe that God alone can win this battle, and therefore we pray for his hand to be in everything we undertake.

NOTES

Chapter 1

[1] Peter Wehner, a senior fellow at the Ethics and Public Policy Center and who served in the previous Republican administrations, speaks of his and others' decision in "Why I Can No Longer Call Myself an Evangelical Republican" in the *New York Times Sunday Review*, 12.10.17, pp. 4-5: "…the support being given by many Republicans and white evangelicals to President Trump and now [Senate candidate] Mr. Moore have caused me to rethink my identification with both groups…Just the other day I received a note from a friend of mine, a pastor who told me that he no longer uses the label 'evangelical' to describe himself, even though he meets every element of its historical definition, 'because the term is now so stained as to ruin my ability to be what evangelicalism was supposed to be'… Institutional renewal and regeneration are possible, and I'm going to push for them. But for now a solid majority of Republicans and self-described evangelicals are firmly aboard the Trump train, which is doing its utmost to give a seat of privilege to Mr. Moore. So for those of us who still think of ourselves as conservative and Christian, it's enough already."

[2] Václav Havel, "Forgetting We Are Not God," *First Things* 51 (March 1995), 48.

[3] "Recent research on Jefferson's letter (including the use of FBI computers to read beneath the ink he used to scratch out some of the original words) has shown that Jefferson was not so much hostile to government engagement with religions as to *federal* sponsorship of religion. Reasoning from Jefferson's scratched out words, Library of Congress archive director James Hutson has argued that this letter 'was never conceived by Jefferson to be a statement of fundamental principles.' Instead, it was a political document designed not to offend the strict separationists while leaving open tacit approval of *state* sponsored religious exercises. While Jefferson thought federal sponsorship of a day of prayer and thanksgiving was inappropriate, as a state governor, he himself called for such observances" (David Neff, "Can I Get a Witness," *Christianity Today* [August 9, 1999]: 26–27). Ironically (and with polarizing effect), Jefferson's tacit endorsement of (local) state-sponsored expressions of faith is sometimes used in our day to forbid

the free expression of faith in public venues. The argument over the proper meaning and application of Jefferson's idea will, no doubt, be with us for some time. Thoughtful people on the left, while admitting that the language is not in the Constitution, assert that the *concept* is foundational to the founders' thinking and is reflected in the First Amendment. And even when everyone agrees regarding the origin of the phrase and the notion that church and state should in some sense be separate, there often remains strong disagreement on what that separation should look like in practical terms.

4 Quoted in Philip Yancey, *Church, Why Bother?* (Grand Rapids, MI: Zondervan, 1998), 94–95.

5 In 1637, for example, Rev. Thomas Shepard described the bloody subjugation of a band of marauding Poquots as a "divine slaughter by the hands of the English." (*The Transplanting of Culture: 1607–1650,* vol. 1)

Chapter 2

6 Columbia professor Randall Balmer documents his defection, for political reasons, from the ranks of evangelicalism in *Thy Kingdom Come: How the Religious Right Distorts Faith and Threatens America* (New York: Basic Books, 2006).

7 James Davison Hunter, *To Change the World* (New York: Oxford University Press, 2010).

8 This phrase is generally attributed to Adam Baker.

9 Jake Halpern, *Fame Junkies: The Hidden Truths Behind America's Favorite Addiction* (New York: Houghton Mifflin, 2007), 207.

10 I am indebted to many, particularly Charles Haynes, for this use of the Golden Rule.

11 See Stephen L. Carter, *The Culture of Disbelief* (New York: Basic Books, 1993), for an excellent critique by a Yale law professor of our culture's tendency to trivialize the role of faith in public life.

Chapter 3

12 Other factors, of course, apply. Change in cultural gatekeepers—newspaper editors, screen writers, educational leaders—is disproportionately influential (See Hunter, *To Change the World.*)

[13] Huge denominations, like the Roman Catholic Church, can perhaps take the risk more easily than independent community churches, since the former are known publicly to embrace a spectrum of opinions, whereas the only thing a stranger will know about the latter will be what he sees when he walks through the door.

[14] E. J. Goodspeed, quoted by William Barclay in *The Gospel of Mark* (Philadelphia: Westminster, 1975), 287.

Chapter 4

[15] Quoted in Christoph Schönborn, "The Hope of Heaven, the Hope of Earth," *First Things* (April 1995), 34.

[16] James I. Packer, *A Quest for Godliness* (Wheaton, IL: Crossway, 1990), 14.

Chapter 5

[17] See Solomon's prayer at the dedication of the temple (1 Kings 8, especially verse 27). Note as well that non-Jews were routinely invited to join the commonwealth of Israel, thus reminding the Jews that, though he had chosen them, Yahweh had never ceased to be the Lord of all people (Numbers 15:13–16).

[18] Lord Acton, quoted by William Barclay in *The Gospel of Mark* (Philadelphia: Westminster, 1975), 286–287.

[19] Quoted in Tim Dowley, ed., *Eerdman's Handbook to the History of Christianity* (Grand Rapids: Eerdmans, 1977), 363.

[20] Augustine, *The City of God*, book XIV, chap. 4, trans. Henry Bettenson (New York: Penguin, 1972), 600.

[21] Daniel M. Bell Jr. discusses this problem in *Just War as Christian Discipleship: Re-centering the Tradition in the Church rather than the State* (Grand Rapids: Brazos Press, 2009)

[22] John Howard Yoder, *The Politics of Jesus* (Grand Rapids: Eerdmans, 1972), 190.

[23] Ibid., 191.

[24] Quoted in Dowley, *Eerdman's Handbook to the History of Christianity* (Grand Rapids: Eerdmans, 1977), 402.

[25] Robert Rodat, 1988. *Saving Private Ryan*, Paramount Pictures. The film

features a platoon of soldiers commissioned shortly after the D-Day invasion to find Private Ryan (the last of four sons, all but him killed in battle) and to bring him safely home to his grief-stricken mother.

[26] Augustine, who believed in the just use of violence, nevertheless grieved that any violence should be necessary: "The wise man…if he remembers that he is a human being…will rather lament the fact that he is faced with the necessity of waging just wars; for if they were not just, he would not have to engage in them, and consequently there would be no wars for a wise man…Everyone who reflects with sorrow on such grievous evils, in all their horror and cruelty, must acknowledge the misery of them" (Augustine, *The City of God,* 861–862).

Chapter 6

[27] While in a Nazi prison, Bonhoeffer wrote a poem entitled "Who am I?" Part of it reads, "Who am I? They often tell me/I used to speak to my warders/Freely and friendly and clearly/As though it were mine to command" (*Letters and Papers from Prison* [New York: Macmillan, 1962], 221).

[28] Jean-Jacques Rousseau, *The Social Contract,* quoted by Christopher Cardinal Schönborn, "Hope of Heaven, Hope of Earth," *First Things* (April 1995), 32.

[29] Charles Colson, *Kingdoms in Conflict* (Grand Rapids: Morrow/Zondervan, 1987), 246.

[30] Quoted in Iain H. Murray, *Jonathan Edwards* (Carlisle, PA: Banner of Truth Trust, 1987), 167.

Chapter 7

[31] Tom Clancy, *The Sum of All Fears* (New York: Berkley, 1991), 18.

[32] Imagine that immediately after his pronouncement about the Roman denarius, Jesus had asked for a baby to be brought to him and, holding it in his arms, had repeated the question, "Whose image is *this*?" The proper, if shocking, answer (straight out of Genesis 1:26) would have been, "It is God's image." And Jesus' rejoinder would have been, "Then give this one fully to God."

[33] Quoted in Schönborn, "Hope of Heaven, Hope of Earth," 32. The philosopher asserts that this divided loyalty leads to "a continuous struggle between the jurisdictions…which has made any reasonable civil order im-

possible in the Christian states." This observation may have had some historical validity at the time, though the success of the American experiment, which Rousseau did not live to see (he died in 1778), provides a notable exception. We noted earlier that loyalty to Christ produces fine citizens.

[34] Edmund Clowney, *The Message of 1 Peter* (Downers Grove, IL: InterVarsity Press, 1988), 109.

[35] Ervin Duggan, "Pluralism That Makes a Difference," *First Things* (April 1995), 58.

[36] "The Theological Clarification of the Present State of the German Evangelical Churches" (1934) in *Bekenntnisschiften und Kirchenordnungen der nach Gottes Wort reformierten Kirche,* ed. W. Niesel (Zurich: Evangelischer Verlag, 1938), 335.25–31; 335:46–336.10.

[37] Mothers with difficult pregnancies are, of course, also our neighbors. The church that condemns abortion fails in her calling if she does not also speak and act with love toward women who are ill equipped to care for their children.

[38] See David Wallace-Wells, *The Uninhabitable Earth: Life after Warming*, for a troubling call to arms as we contemplate where our neglect regarding climate change is likely to bring us and our children.

[39] The Alabama State Legislature passed such a law with this aim in view in May, 2019, echoing similar efforts in Arkansas, Georgia, Kentucky, Mississippi, Missouri, Ohio, and Utah.

[40] From "Debate on Mr. Wilberforce's Resolutions respecting the Slave Trade" in William Cobbett, *The Parliamentary History of England* (London: T. Curson Hansard, 1806-1820), vol. 28 (1789-91), columns 41–42.

[41] The source for my account of Wilberforce's battle against slavery is Colson, *Kingdoms in Conflict,* 102–108.

[42] The great evangelist John Wesley had written to Wilberforce, "Unless the Divine power has raised you up as *Athanasius contra mundum,* I see not how you can go through your glorious enterprise in opposing that execrable villainy, which is the scandal of religion, of England, and of human nature...Oh, be not weary in well doing. Go on in the name of God, and in the power of His might." (Quoted in Colson, *Kingdoms in Conflict,* 105).

Chapter 8

[43] Charles Drew, letter to the editor, *The Boston Globe,* October 22, 1979.

[44] Edmund Clowney, *The Message of 1 Peter* (Downers Grove, IL: Inter-Varsity Press, 1988), 105. Clowney writes: "Many interpreters give another meaning to the word for 'creature.' They take it to mean 'order' or 'institution.' (The NIV expands this to 'authority instituted.') It is hard to find a clear example of this meaning outside the Bible, and it never means this in biblical usage. Peter is not talking about submission to institutions, but submission to people; to people, however, who have been given roles to fill in God's appointment. Our submission is to creatures of God made in his image."

[45] Quoted in Paul Johnson, *Modern Times* (New York, NY: Harper and Row, 1983), 70.

[46] Ibid., 70.

[47] C. S. Lewis, *The Weight of Glory* (Grand Rapids, MI.: Eerdmans, 1972), 15.

[48] Clowney, *The Message of 1 Peter*, 111.

[49] James Davison Hunter, *Before the Shooting Begins* (New York: The Free Press, 1994), 232.

[50] James Thomas Flexner, *Washington: The Indispensable Man* (New York: Little, Brown, 1969), 207.

[51] Ibid., 210.

[52] Ibid., 217–218.

[53] Colson, *Kingdoms in Conflict.* The accounts of Eckerd and Ferrell appear on pp. 262–263 and pp. 255–257.

[54] Ibid., 256.

Chapter 9

[55] Quoted in David P. Gushee, "Following Jesus to the Gallows," *Christianity Today*, April 3, 1995, 30.

[56] Martin Luther King Jr., *Autobiography* (New York: Warner, 1998), 87–88.

[57] Christine Gardner, "Slave Redemption," *Christianity Today*, August 9, 1999, 28.

Appendix A

58 Signers of the Charter include, but are not limited to, presidents Jimmy Carter and Gerald Ford, chief justices William Rehnquist and Warren Burger, senators Mark O. Hatfield and Daniel Patrick Moynihan, Nat Hentoff (columnist for *The Washington Post* and *The Village Voice*), Richard Neuhaus (director, Center for Religion and Society), Frank Fahrenkopf Jr. (chairman, Republican National Committee), Paul Kirk Jr. (chairman, Democratic National Committee), professors Peter Berger (Boston University) and William Van Alstyne (Duke University Law School), the Very Reverend Leonid Kishkovsky (president-elect, National Council of Churches), Rabbi Gilbert Klaperman (president, Synagogue Council of America), Archbishop John L. May (president, U. S. Catholic Conference), Imam Warith Deen Muhammad (Muslim American Community Assistance Fund), Adrian Rogers (president, Southern Baptist Convention), John H. White (president, National Association of Evangelicals), Elie Wiesel (Nobel laureate), Bishop Seigen H. Yamaoka (Buddhist Church of America), Donald Seibert (former chairman, J. C. Penney), Walter Cronkite, Coretta Scott King, Kyo Jhin (chairman, Asian-American Voters' Coalition), Derek Bok (president, Harvard University), Frank Rhodes (president, Cornell University), Albert Shanker (president, American Federation of Teachers), Wallace Jorgenson (chairman of the joint boards, National Association of Broadcasters), Horace Deets (Executive Director, American Association of Retired Persons), Frances Hesselbein (national executive director, Girl Scouts of the U.S.A.), Ben H. Love (chief scout executive, Boy Scouts of America), William Aramony (president, United Way of America), James Osborne (national commander, Salvation Army), Carmi Schwartz (executive vice president, Council of Jewish Federations).